The Jobless Era

John McKinsey

1

The Rise of Automation

1.1 The Impact of Technology on Jobs

Technology has always played a significant role in shaping the job market. From the Industrial Revolution to the present day, advancements in technology have revolutionized the way we work and have had a profound impact on the labor force. In recent years, however, the pace of technological change has accelerated, leading to concerns about the future of jobs and the rise of automation.

The Evolution of Automation

Automation, the use of technology to perform tasks that were previously done by humans, has been a driving force behind the changing nature of work. It has transformed industries, increased productivity, and improved efficiency. The impact of automation can be seen across various sectors, from manufacturing to service industries.

Automation in Manufacturing

One of the most significant areas where automation has had a profound impact is manufacturing. The

● ● ●

introduction of machines and robotics has revolutionized production processes, leading to increased output and reduced costs. Tasks that were once performed by human workers, such as assembly line work, have been taken over by machines capable of performing repetitive tasks with precision and speed.

While automation has undoubtedly brought numerous benefits to the manufacturing sector, it has also resulted in job displacement. Many low-skilled jobs have been replaced by machines, leading to unemployment and a shift in the required skill set for workers. This has created a challenge for individuals who were previously employed in these roles and now find themselves without work.

Automation in Service Industries

Automation has also made its way into service industries, transforming the way we interact with businesses and consume services. From self-checkout machines in supermarkets to automated customer service systems, technology has streamlined processes and reduced the need for human intervention.

In the banking sector, for example, the rise of online banking and mobile applications has made it possible for customers to perform transactions and access services without the need for physical branches or tellers. This shift has led to a decrease in the demand for traditional banking jobs, such as bank tellers, and an increase in the need for individuals with digital skills to support these technological advancements.

●●●

The impact of automation on jobs is a topic of great debate. While automation has undoubtedly led to job displacement in certain sectors, it has also created new opportunities and transformed the nature of work. The benefits of automation include increased productivity, improved efficiency, and the ability to perform tasks that are dangerous or physically demanding for humans.

Automation has also led to the creation of new jobs in industries that support and develop technology. The demand for individuals with skills in programming, data analysis, and artificial intelligence has increased significantly. As technology continues to advance, there will be a growing need for individuals who can understand, operate, and maintain these automated systems.

However, the rapid pace of technological change has raised concerns about the future of work. Many fear that automation will lead to widespread job loss and unemployment, particularly for low-skilled workers. The fear is that machines will be able to perform tasks more efficiently and at a lower cost than humans, making certain jobs obsolete.

Furthermore, the impact of automation is not evenly distributed across industries and regions. Some sectors may experience significant job losses, while others may see job growth. This can lead to income inequality and wealth disparity, as those who are unable to adapt to the changing job market may struggle to find employment or may be forced into lower-paying jobs.

In conclusion, the impact of technology and automation on jobs is undeniable. While automation has brought numerous benefits, such as increased productivity and efficiency, it has also led to job displacement and concerns about the future of work. As we move forward into the jobless era, it is crucial to understand the implications of automation and find ways to adapt and thrive in a changing job market.

1.2 Automation in Manufacturing

Automation has revolutionized the manufacturing industry, transforming the way goods are produced and impacting the workforce in profound ways. The rise of automation in manufacturing has brought about significant changes, both positive and negative, that have reshaped the job landscape.

The Evolution of Automation in Manufacturing

Manufacturing has always been at the forefront of technological advancements, and automation is no exception. Over the years, we have witnessed a gradual shift from manual labor to automated processes in factories and production lines. This transition has been driven by the desire for increased efficiency, productivity, and cost-effectiveness.

Early forms of automation in manufacturing can be traced back to the Industrial Revolution, with the introduction of machinery and steam-powered

● ● ●

systems. However, it was the advent of computer technology and the development of programmable logic controllers (PLCs) that truly revolutionized the industry. These advancements allowed for the automation of complex tasks and processes, leading to higher precision and faster production rates.

Benefits of Automation in Manufacturing

Automation in manufacturing offers numerous benefits that have contributed to its widespread adoption. One of the primary advantages is increased productivity. Automated systems can work tirelessly, 24/7, without the need for breaks or rest, resulting in higher output and reduced production time. This increased efficiency leads to cost savings for manufacturers and potentially lower prices for consumers.

Moreover, automation has improved product quality and consistency. By removing the human element from repetitive tasks, the chances of errors and defects are significantly reduced. Automated systems can perform tasks with precision and accuracy, ensuring that each product meets the desired specifications. This level of consistency is crucial, particularly in industries where precision is paramount, such as aerospace or medical device manufacturing.

Automation also enhances workplace safety. By replacing humans in hazardous or physically demanding tasks, the risk of accidents and injuries is minimized. Robots and automated machinery can handle heavy lifting, repetitive motions, and exposure to dangerous substances without endangering human workers. This not only protects employees but also reduces the financial burden on companies in terms of workers' compensation and insurance costs.

Impact on the Workforce

While automation brings undeniable benefits, it also poses challenges for the workforce. The introduction of automated systems in manufacturing has led to a decrease in the demand for certain types of jobs. Tasks that were once performed by humans are now handled by machines, resulting in job displacement and unemployment for many workers.

The most affected group is often the low-skilled workers who perform repetitive and routine tasks. These jobs are easily automated, as machines can perform them more efficiently and at a lower cost. As a result, individuals in these roles may find themselves without employment or forced to seek alternative employment opportunities.

However, it is important to note that automation does not necessarily lead to a complete elimination of jobs. Instead, it tends to shift the nature of work. While some jobs may disappear, new roles emerge to support and maintain the automated systems. These positions often require higher levels of technical skills and expertise, creating a demand for a more skilled workforce.

The Role of Humans in Automated Manufacturing

Despite the increasing presence of automation in manufacturing, humans still play a vital role in the

● ● ●

industry. While machines excel at repetitive and precise tasks, they lack the adaptability, problem-solving abilities, and creativity that humans possess. This has led to a shift in the types of jobs available, with a greater emphasis on roles that require critical thinking, problem-solving, and creativity.

Human workers are essential in areas such as design, innovation, quality control, and maintenance of automated systems. They bring a unique perspective and the ability to think outside the box, which is crucial for driving innovation and continuous improvement in manufacturing processes. Additionally, humans are better equipped to handle non-routine tasks that require flexibility and adaptability.

To thrive in an automated manufacturing environment, workers need to acquire new skills and adapt to the changing job landscape. This may involve upskilling or reskilling to meet the demands of the evolving industry. By embracing lifelong learning and acquiring new competencies, individuals can position themselves for success in the job market of the future.

Conclusion

Automation has revolutionized the manufacturing industry, bringing about increased productivity, improved product quality, and enhanced workplace safety. However, it has also resulted in job displacement and a shift in the types of jobs available. While automation may eliminate certain roles, it also creates new opportunities that require higher levels of skills and expertise. The key to thriving in an automated

● ● ●

manufacturing era lies in embracing change, acquiring new skills, and leveraging the unique abilities that humans bring to the table.

1.3 Automation in Service Industries

Automation has not only revolutionized the manufacturing sector but has also made significant inroads into service industries. From customer service to healthcare, automation has transformed the way these industries operate, leading to increased efficiency and productivity. In this section, we will explore the impact of automation on service industries and discuss the benefits and challenges it presents.

The Changing Landscape of Service Industries

Service industries encompass a wide range of sectors, including retail, hospitality, finance, healthcare, and customer service. Traditionally, these industries heavily relied on human labor to deliver their services. However, with advancements in technology, automation has become a game-changer.

One of the most notable examples of automation in service industries is the rise of chatbots and virtual assistants in customer service. These intelligent systems can handle customer inquiries, provide support, and even process transactions, reducing the need for human intervention. This not only saves time but also improves customer satisfaction by providing instant and accurate responses.

In the healthcare sector, automation has revolutionized various aspects of patient care. Robotic surgery systems have made complex surgeries more precise and less invasive, leading to faster recovery times and improved patient outcomes. Additionally, automated systems for medication dispensing and record-keeping have streamlined administrative tasks, allowing healthcare professionals to focus more on patient care.

Benefits of Automation in Service Industries

Automation in service industries offers several benefits that contribute to increased efficiency and improved customer experiences. Firstly, automated systems can operate 24/7 without the need for breaks or vacations, ensuring round-the-clock service availability. This is particularly advantageous in industries such as customer service and hospitality, where customers expect immediate assistance at any time.

Secondly, automation reduces the potential for human error. Machines can perform repetitive tasks with precision and accuracy, minimizing the risk of mistakes that can occur due to fatigue or distraction. This is especially crucial in sectors like finance and healthcare, where even a small error can have significant consequences.

Furthermore, automation allows businesses to reallocate human resources to more complex and creative tasks. By automating routine and mundane activities, employees can focus on activities that require critical thinking, problem-solving, and innovation. This not only enhances job satisfaction but also drives innovation and growth within organizations.

Challenges and Concerns

While automation brings numerous benefits, it also presents challenges and concerns that need to be addressed. One of the primary concerns is the potential displacement of human workers. As automation continues to advance, there is a fear that many jobs in service industries will become obsolete, leading to unemployment and economic inequality.

Another challenge is the need for upskilling and reskilling the workforce. As automation takes over routine tasks, employees must acquire new skills to remain relevant in the job market. This requires a significant investment in training and education to ensure that workers can adapt to the changing demands of the industry.

Additionally, there are concerns about the impact of automation on the quality of service. While automated systems can handle many tasks efficiently, they may lack the human touch and empathy that customers often seek. This raises questions about the balance between automation and maintaining a personalized customer experience.

Striking a Balance

To navigate the challenges and harness the benefits of automation in service industries, a balanced approach is crucial. It is essential to find a middle ground where automation complements human capabilities rather than replacing them entirely. This can be achieved by identifying tasks that can be automated without compromising the quality of service or customer experience.

Moreover, organizations must prioritize the well-being of their employees during the transition to automation. This includes providing opportunities for upskilling and reskilling, ensuring job security, and creating a supportive work environment that encourages innovation and creativity.

Government and policymakers also play a vital role in shaping the future of automation in service industries. They need to develop policies that promote a smooth transition, protect workers' rights, and address the potential social and economic implications of automation.

Conclusion

Automation has brought significant changes to service industries, revolutionizing the way they operate and deliver services. While there are concerns about job displacement and the impact on the quality of service, automation offers numerous benefits, including increased efficiency, improved customer experiences, and the opportunity for employees to focus on more complex tasks. By striking a balance between automation and human capabilities, we can create a future where technology and human skills work hand in hand to drive innovation and growth in service industries.

• • •

1.4 The Pros and Cons of Automation

Automation has undoubtedly revolutionized the way we live and work. It has brought about significant advancements in various industries, making processes faster, more efficient, and less prone to errors. However, like any technological advancement, automation also has its pros and cons. In this section, we will explore the advantages and disadvantages of automation in the job market.

1.4.1 Increased Efficiency and Productivity

One of the most significant advantages of automation is the increased efficiency and productivity it brings to industries. Automated systems can perform tasks at a much faster rate than humans, reducing the time required to complete a task. This not only leads to higher productivity but also allows businesses to meet customer demands more effectively.

Automation also minimizes the risk of errors and inconsistencies that can occur due to human factors. Machines are programmed to perform tasks with precision, reducing the likelihood of mistakes. This can be particularly beneficial in industries where accuracy is crucial, such as manufacturing and healthcare.

1.4.2 Cost Reduction

Another advantage of automation is the potential for cost reduction. While the initial investment in automation technology can be significant, the long-term benefits often outweigh the costs. Automated systems

● ● ●

can replace multiple human workers, reducing labor costs for businesses. Additionally, machines do not require benefits, sick leave, or vacations, further reducing expenses for employers.

Automation can also lead to cost savings through improved resource management. Machines can optimize the use of materials, energy, and time, resulting in reduced waste and increased efficiency. This can have a positive impact on the environment as well, as automation can help minimize resource consumption and carbon emissions.

1.4.3 Enhanced Safety

Automation has the potential to improve workplace safety by reducing the exposure of workers to hazardous conditions. Dangerous tasks can be assigned to machines, minimizing the risk of accidents and injuries. For example, in manufacturing industries, robots can handle heavy machinery and perform tasks in high-risk environments, keeping human workers out of harm's way.

Automated systems can also be equipped with sensors and safety features to detect potential dangers and respond accordingly. This proactive approach to safety can help prevent accidents and protect workers from harm. By reducing workplace injuries, automation contributes to a healthier and more secure work environment.

1.4.4 Job Displacement and Unemployment

While automation offers numerous benefits, it also raises concerns about job displacement and unemployment. As machines take over tasks previously performed by humans, there is a risk of job loss in certain industries. This can lead to unemployment and economic instability for individuals and communities that heavily rely on those jobs.

The fear of job displacement is not unfounded. Studies have shown that automation has already replaced many jobs, particularly in manufacturing and routine-based tasks. As technology continues to advance, more jobs are at risk of being automated, including those in service industries and even professions that were once considered safe from automation.

1.4.5 Skill Shift and Job Creation

While automation may eliminate certain jobs, it also creates new opportunities and shifts the demand for skills. As machines take over repetitive and mundane tasks, there is a growing need for workers with advanced technical skills to operate and maintain automated systems. This shift in skill requirements opens up new avenues for employment and career growth.

Automation also has the potential to create entirely new industries and job roles. As technology evolves, new products and services emerge, leading to the creation of jobs that were previously unimaginable. For example, the rise of artificial intelligence has given birth to fields such as data science and machine learning, which require specialized knowledge and expertise.

1.4.6 Economic Impact and Income Inequality

The widespread adoption of automation can have a significant impact on the economy as a whole. While automation can lead to increased productivity and cost reduction for businesses, it can also contribute to income inequality. The benefits of automation are often concentrated in the hands of business owners and shareholders, while workers may face job insecurity and stagnant wages.

Furthermore, automation can exacerbate existing income disparities by widening the gap between high-skilled and low-skilled workers. Those with the necessary skills to thrive in an automated world may enjoy higher wages and better job prospects, while others may struggle to find meaningful employment. This can lead to social unrest and economic inequality if not addressed effectively.

1.4.7 Ethical Considerations

Automation also raises important ethical considerations. As machines become more intelligent and capable, questions arise about the ethical use of automation and artificial intelligence. Issues such as privacy, data security, and the potential for bias and discrimination need to be carefully addressed to ensure fairness and equity in an automated society.

Additionally, the ethical implications of job displacement and unemployment cannot be ignored. Society must grapple with the question of how to support individuals who have lost their jobs due to automation. This includes providing retraining opportunities, social safety nets, and exploring alternative economic models such as universal basic income.

In conclusion, automation brings both advantages and disadvantages to the job market. While it enhances efficiency, productivity, and safety, it also poses challenges such as job displacement, income inequality, and ethical concerns. As we navigate the jobless era, it is crucial to strike a balance between embracing automation's benefits and mitigating its negative impacts to create a future that benefits all members of society.

2

The Changing Nature of Work

2.1 The Gig Economy

In recent years, the world has witnessed a significant shift in the way people work. The rise of the gig economy has revolutionized the traditional employment landscape, offering individuals a new way to earn a living. The gig economy refers to a labor market characterized by the prevalence of short-term contracts or freelance work, as opposed to permanent employment. This emerging trend has been fueled by advancements in technology, changing societal attitudes, and the desire for greater flexibility and autonomy in work.

The Rise of Gig Work

The gig economy has gained momentum due to several factors. One of the key drivers is the rapid advancement of digital platforms and online marketplaces that connect workers with employers. These platforms have made it easier than ever for individuals to offer their services and find work opportunities. Whether it's driving for a ride-sharing service, delivering groceries, or providing freelance graphic design services, the gig economy offers a wide range of options for workers across various industries.

Another factor contributing to the rise of gig work is the changing preferences and expectations of the workforce. Many individuals are seeking more control over their work-life balance and are drawn to the flexibility and freedom that gig work provides. This shift in mindset has led to a growing number of people opting for gig work as a means of earning income while pursuing other interests or personal goals.

Benefits and Challenges

The gig economy offers several benefits for both workers and employers. For workers, it provides the opportunity to have a more flexible schedule, choose the projects they want to work on, and be their own boss. This level of autonomy can be particularly appealing to those who value independence and prefer to work on their own terms. Additionally, gig work can provide a source of income during periods of unemployment or underemployment, offering a safety net for individuals in uncertain economic times.

Employers also benefit from the gig economy as it allows them to tap into a diverse pool of talent on an as-needed basis. They can access specialized skills and expertise without the long-term commitment and costs associated with hiring full-time employees. This flexibility enables businesses to adapt quickly to changing market demands and scale their workforce accordingly.

However, the gig economy is not without its challenges. One of the main concerns is the lack of employment benefits and protections typically associated with traditional employment. Gig workers often do not receive benefits such as health insurance, retirement plans, or paid time off. Additionally, the unpredictable nature of gig work can lead to income instability and financial insecurity for some individuals. Without the stability of a steady paycheck, gig workers may struggle to plan for the future or meet their financial obligations.

The Future of Work

As the gig economy continues to grow, it is reshaping the future of work. Traditional notions of employment are being challenged, and the concept of a lifelong career with a single employer is becoming less common. Instead, individuals are embracing a more fluid and dynamic approach to work, moving between different gigs and projects throughout their careers.

The gig economy also presents opportunities for individuals to develop a diverse set of skills and experiences. With each new gig, workers have the chance to learn and adapt, gaining valuable insights and knowledge that can enhance their employability. This constant learning and upskilling are becoming essential in a rapidly changing job market, where technological advancements and automation are reshaping the skills required for various roles.

Furthermore, the gig economy has the potential to foster entrepreneurship and innovation. Many gig workers are independent contractors who have the freedom to pursue their own business ventures alongside their gig work. This entrepreneurial spirit can lead to the creation of new products, services, and job opportunities, driving economic growth and innovation.

In conclusion, the gig economy is transforming the way we work, offering individuals greater flexibility and autonomy in their careers. While it presents numerous benefits, such as flexibility and access to a diverse range of talent for employers, it also poses challenges related to income stability and lack of employment benefits. As the gig economy continues to evolve, it is crucial for policymakers, businesses, and workers to address these challenges and ensure that the future of work is inclusive, fair, and sustainable.

2.2 Remote Work and Telecommuting

In the ever-evolving landscape of work, remote work and telecommuting have emerged as significant trends that are reshaping the way we think about traditional employment. With advancements in technology and the increasing connectivity of the world, the concept of being physically present in an office is no longer a necessity for many professionals. Remote work and telecommuting offer individuals the freedom to work from anywhere, breaking down geographical barriers and providing a range of benefits for both employees and employers.

The Rise of Remote Work

Remote work, also known as telework or telecommuting, refers to the practice of working outside of a traditional office environment. This can involve working from home, a co-working space, or any other location that suits the individual's needs. The rise of remote work can be attributed to several factors, including technological advancements, changing attitudes towards work-life balance, and the increasing demand for flexibility in the workplace.

Advantages of Remote Work

Remote work offers numerous advantages for both employees and employers. For employees, the ability to work remotely provides a greater level of flexibility and autonomy. It eliminates the need for long commutes, reduces stress associated with rush hour traffic, and allows individuals to create a work environment that suits their preferences. Remote work also enables a better work-life balance, as it allows individuals to spend more time with their families, pursue personal interests, and maintain a healthier lifestyle.

Employers also benefit from remote work arrangements. By embracing remote work, companies can tap into a global talent pool, accessing skilled professionals from different parts of the world. This expands the potential for innovation and diversity within the workforce. Remote work also reduces overhead costs for employers, as they no longer need to provide physical office spaces for all employees. Additionally, studies have shown that remote workers are often more productive and experience higher job satisfaction, leading to increased employee retention.

Overcoming Challenges

While remote work offers numerous advantages, it is not without its challenges. One of the primary concerns for employers is ensuring effective communication and collaboration among remote teams. However, advancements in communication technology, such as video conferencing, instant messaging, and project management tools, have made it easier than ever to bridge the gap between remote workers. Regular check-ins, virtual meetings, and clear communication channels are essential for maintaining a cohesive and productive remote team.

For employees, one of the challenges of remote work is maintaining a healthy work-life balance. Without clear boundaries between work and personal life, it can be easy to blur the lines and find oneself working longer hours. Establishing a dedicated workspace, setting clear work hours, and practicing self-discipline are crucial for maintaining a healthy work-life balance while working remotely.

The Future of Remote Work

As technology continues to advance and the world becomes increasingly interconnected, remote work is expected to become even more prevalent in the future. The COVID-19 pandemic has accelerated the adoption of remote work, with many companies realizing the benefits and feasibility of remote work arrangements.

● ● ●

This shift has led to a reevaluation of traditional office spaces and a greater emphasis on flexible work options.

The future of remote work also holds the potential for increased collaboration and innovation. As remote teams become the norm, companies are investing in tools and platforms that facilitate seamless communication and collaboration. Virtual reality and augmented reality technologies may further enhance remote collaboration, allowing individuals to feel as if they are physically present in the same space, regardless of their geographical location.

Conclusion

Remote work and telecommuting have revolutionized the way we approach work, offering individuals the freedom to work from anywhere and providing numerous benefits for both employees and employers. The rise of remote work has been driven by technological advancements, changing attitudes towards work-life balance, and the need for flexibility in the workplace. While there are challenges to overcome, such as effective communication and maintaining work-life balance, the future of remote work looks promising. As we continue to embrace the possibilities of remote work, we can create a more inclusive, flexible, and productive work environment for all.

2.3 The Rise of Freelancing

In the ever-evolving landscape of work, one trend that has gained significant traction is the rise of freelancing. As traditional employment models continue to shift, more and more individuals are embracing the freedom and flexibility that comes with being a freelancer. This chapter explores the rise of freelancing, its impact on the job market, and the opportunities and challenges it presents.

The Evolution of Freelancing

Freelancing is not a new concept. It has been around for centuries, with artisans, craftsmen, and professionals offering their services independently. However, in recent years, advancements in technology and changes in the global economy have propelled the freelance economy to new heights.

The digital revolution has played a pivotal role in the rise of freelancing. The internet has made it easier than ever for individuals to connect with clients and showcase their skills and expertise. Online platforms and marketplaces have emerged, providing freelancers with a vast array of opportunities across various industries and sectors.

The Benefits of Freelancing

Freelancing offers numerous benefits that have contributed to its growing popularity. One of the primary advantages is the freedom and flexibility it provides. Freelancers have the autonomy to choose their projects, set their own schedules, and work from anywhere in the world. This level of control over their work-life balance is highly appealing to many individuals.

Additionally, freelancers have the opportunity to diversify their income streams. By working on multiple projects for different clients, they can mitigate the risk of relying on a single employer. This flexibility allows freelancers to adapt to changing market demands and explore new opportunities.

The Challenges of Freelancing

While freelancing offers many advantages, it also presents its fair share of challenges. One of the main difficulties freelancers face is the lack of job security. Unlike traditional employees, freelancers do not have the stability of a steady paycheck or benefits such as health insurance and retirement plans. They must navigate the uncertainties of the gig economy and constantly seek new projects to sustain their income.

Another challenge is the need for self-discipline and self-motivation. Freelancers are responsible for managing their time, meeting deadlines, and ensuring the quality of their work. Without the structure and accountability of a traditional workplace, it can be easy to succumb to distractions or procrastination.

The Gig Economy and Freelancing

The rise of freelancing is closely intertwined with the emergence of the gig economy. The gig economy refers to a labor market characterized by short-term contracts or freelance work as opposed to permanent employment. It encompasses a wide range of industries, from ride-sharing services to creative freelancers.

Freelancing has become a significant component of the gig economy, with individuals leveraging their skills and expertise to offer services on a project basis. This shift in the employment landscape has been driven by various factors, including the desire for flexibility, the pursuit of work-life balance, and the changing needs of businesses.

The Future of Freelancing

As technology continues to advance and the nature of work evolves, the future of freelancing looks promising. The gig economy is projected to grow even further, with more individuals opting for freelance work as their primary source of income. The ability to work remotely and the increasing demand for specialized skills are driving this trend.

Furthermore, the rise of automation and artificial intelligence is expected to create new opportunities for freelancers. As certain tasks become automated, individuals will need to focus on areas that require human creativity, critical thinking, and problem-solving skills. Freelancers, with their ability to adapt and offer specialized services, are well-positioned to thrive in this changing landscape.

Conclusion

The rise of freelancing is a testament to the evolving nature of work in the modern era. It offers individuals the freedom to pursue their passions, control over their schedules, and the opportunity to diversify their income. However, freelancing also comes with its own set of challenges, including job insecurity and the need for self-discipline.

As the gig economy continues to expand and technology reshapes industries, freelancing is likely to play an increasingly significant role in the job market. Embracing the opportunities and addressing the challenges of freelancing will be crucial for individuals seeking to thrive in the jobless era.

2.4 The Future of Work

The future of work is a topic that has been widely discussed and debated in recent years. As technology continues to advance at an unprecedented rate, the way we work is undergoing a significant transformation. The rise of automation, artificial intelligence, and other technological advancements are reshaping the job market and raising questions about the future of employment.

2.4.1 The Impact of Automation

Automation has already had a profound impact on various industries, and its influence is only expected to grow in the coming years. Many routine and repetitive tasks that were once performed by humans are now being automated, leading to increased efficiency and productivity. However, this automation also raises concerns about job displacement and the potential for widespread unemployment.

2.4.2 The Rise of Artificial Intelligence

Artificial intelligence (AI) is another technological advancement that is poised to reshape the future of work. AI systems are becoming increasingly sophisticated, capable of performing complex tasks that were once thought to be exclusive to human intelligence. From self-driving cars to virtual assistants, AI is revolutionizing various industries and changing the way we work.

2.4.3 The Gig Economy and Freelancing

The gig economy and freelancing have gained significant traction in recent years, offering individuals the opportunity to work on a project-by-project basis rather than being tied to a traditional 9-to-5 job. This shift towards more flexible work arrangements has been facilitated by advancements in technology, allowing individuals to connect with clients and customers from anywhere in the world. However, the gig economy also presents challenges such as job insecurity and lack of benefits.

2.4.4 The Role of Humans in the Future of Work

While automation and AI are undoubtedly transforming the job market, it is important to recognize the unique skills and abilities that humans bring to the table. As technology takes over routine tasks, there is an increasing demand for skills that are uniquely human, such as creativity, critical thinking, emotional intelligence, and problem-solving. These skills are difficult to replicate with technology, making them highly valuable in the future of work.

2.4.5 The Need for Lifelong Learning

As the nature of work continues to evolve, it is crucial for individuals to embrace lifelong learning. The skills required in the job market are constantly changing, and individuals must be willing to adapt and acquire new skills to remain relevant. Continuous learning and upskilling will be essential for individuals to thrive in the future of work.

2.4.6 The Importance of Collaboration and Adaptability

In a rapidly changing work environment, collaboration and adaptability will be key to success. As technology continues to advance, new job roles and industries will emerge, requiring individuals to work together and adapt to new ways of working. The ability to collaborate effectively with both humans and machines will be crucial in the future of work.

2.4.7 Redefining Work-Life Balance

The future of work also calls for a redefinition of work-life balance. With the ability to work remotely and the blurring of boundaries between work and personal life, it is important to find a balance that allows individuals to thrive both professionally and personally. This may involve setting boundaries, prioritizing self-care, and finding ways to disconnect from work when needed.

2.4.8 The Role of Government and Policies

As the job market continues to evolve, governments and policymakers will play a crucial role in shaping the future of work. They will need to develop policies that address the challenges posed by automation and AI, such as job displacement and income inequality. Additionally, governments may need to explore new social safety nets, such as universal basic income, to ensure that individuals have access to the resources they need in a jobless era.

In conclusion, the future of work is undoubtedly being shaped by automation, AI, and other technological advancements. While these changes may lead to job displacement and challenges, they also present opportunities for individuals to develop new skills and embrace new ways of working. Collaboration, adaptability, and lifelong learning will be key to thriving in the future of work. Governments and policymakers also have a crucial role to play in ensuring a fair and equitable transition to a jobless era. By embracing change and creating a positive future, we can navigate the challenges and embrace the opportunities that lie ahead.

3

The Jobless Society

3.1 Unemployment and its Consequences

Unemployment is a pressing issue that has far-reaching consequences for individuals, communities, and societies as a whole. As automation and technological advancements continue to reshape the job market, the number of jobless individuals is on the rise. This chapter explores the various consequences of unemployment and the challenges it poses to our society.

The Economic Impact of Unemployment

Unemployment has significant economic implications. When individuals are unable to find work, they are unable to contribute to the economy through their purchasing power. This lack of consumer spending can lead to a decrease in demand for goods and services, which in turn can result in reduced production and layoffs in other sectors. The ripple effect of unemployment can create a downward spiral, leading to further job losses and economic instability.

Furthermore, unemployment places a burden on government resources. As jobless individuals seek financial assistance through unemployment benefits and other social welfare programs, the government must allocate a significant portion of its budget to support them. This strain on public finances can limit the government's ability to invest in other areas such as infrastructure, education, and healthcare.

Social Consequences of Unemployment

Unemployment not only affects individuals financially but also has profound social consequences. Joblessness can lead to feelings of isolation, low self-esteem, and a loss of purpose. The lack of a daily routine and the absence of social interactions that come with employment can contribute to mental health issues such as depression and anxiety.

Unemployment can also strain relationships and lead to family tensions. Financial stress and the inability to meet basic needs can create conflicts within households. Moreover, the loss of a job can disrupt social networks and support systems, making it more challenging for individuals to find new opportunities or seek emotional support.

Health Implications

The impact of unemployment on physical and mental health cannot be overlooked. Studies have shown that joblessness is associated with higher rates of chronic illnesses, including cardiovascular disease, diabetes, and obesity. The stress and anxiety caused by

● ● ●

unemployment can weaken the immune system and increase the risk of developing health problems.

Additionally, the loss of employer-provided health insurance can leave individuals without access to necessary medical care. This lack of healthcare coverage can further exacerbate health issues and create barriers to seeking treatment.

Increased Crime Rates

Unemployment has been linked to an increase in crime rates. When individuals are unable to find legitimate employment, some may turn to illegal activities as a means of survival. Desperation and financial strain can push individuals towards engaging in criminal behavior, leading to a rise in theft, drug-related offenses, and other illicit activities.

Moreover, the social unrest caused by high unemployment rates can create an environment conducive to civil unrest and political instability. Unemployment can fuel social tensions and contribute to social unrest, as individuals become frustrated with the lack of opportunities and the widening wealth gap.

Long-Term Consequences

The consequences of unemployment can extend beyond the immediate impact on individuals and communities. Prolonged periods of joblessness can lead to long-term structural changes in the labor market. As technology continues to advance, certain jobs may become obsolete, leaving individuals with outdated skills and limited prospects for reemployment.

Furthermore, the longer individuals remain unemployed, the more difficult it becomes for them to reenter the workforce. Gaps in employment history and a lack of recent experience can make it challenging to compete with other job seekers. This can perpetuate a cycle of unemployment and create a class of individuals who are chronically jobless.

Conclusion

Unemployment is a complex issue with wide-ranging consequences. It not only affects individuals' financial well-being but also has significant social, health, and economic implications. Addressing the challenges posed by joblessness requires a comprehensive approach that includes reimagining education and training, implementing social safety nets, and fostering an environment that promotes entrepreneurship and innovation. Only by understanding and addressing the consequences of unemployment can we strive towards creating a more inclusive and resilient society.

3.2 Income Inequality and Wealth Disparity

As we delve deeper into the jobless era, one of the most pressing issues that arises is income inequality and wealth disparity. With the rise of automation and the decline of traditional employment, the distribution of wealth becomes increasingly skewed, leaving many individuals and communities struggling to make ends meet. In this section, we will explore the causes and consequences of income inequality and wealth disparity in a jobless society.

The Growing Gap

In a jobless society, the gap between the rich and the poor widens significantly. As automation takes over many jobs, those who own and control the technology and capital reap the benefits, while the majority of the population faces unemployment or underemployment. This concentration of wealth in the hands of a few exacerbates income inequality, leading to a society where a small fraction of the population holds a disproportionate amount of wealth and power.

Technological Divide

The advent of automation and advanced technologies further deepens the divide between the haves and the have-nots. Those who possess the necessary skills and education to adapt to the changing job market have a better chance of securing high-paying jobs or creating their own opportunities. However, individuals who lack access to quality education or the means to acquire new skills are left behind, trapped in a cycle of poverty and limited economic prospects.

Disruption of Traditional Industries

Automation disrupts traditional industries, leading to the displacement of workers and the erosion of job security. As machines and algorithms replace human labor, many individuals find themselves without a source of income. This disruption is particularly felt in sectors such as manufacturing and service industries, where routine tasks are easily automated. The loss of jobs in these sectors contributes to income inequality and wealth disparity, as those who were once employed in stable, well-paying jobs are forced into lower-paying, less secure positions.

Impact on Social Mobility

Income inequality and wealth disparity have a profound impact on social mobility. In a jobless society, the ability to move up the socioeconomic ladder becomes increasingly difficult for those who are already disadvantaged. Without access to stable employment and the opportunity to accumulate wealth, individuals and communities are trapped in a cycle of poverty, with limited avenues for upward mobility. This lack of social mobility not only perpetuates income inequality but also hampers overall economic growth and social cohesion.

Strains on Social Welfare Systems

The widening income gap places significant strains on social welfare systems. As unemployment rates rise and income levels stagnate for a large portion of the population, the demand for social assistance programs increases. However, the resources available to support those in need become increasingly limited. This strain on social welfare systems further exacerbates income inequality, as those who are unable to access adequate support are left to bear the brunt of the economic hardships.

Political and Social Unrest

Income inequality and wealth disparity can have far-reaching political and social consequences. When a significant portion of the population feels marginalized and excluded from economic opportunities, it can lead to political unrest, social upheaval, and a breakdown of trust in institutions. The frustration and disillusionment that arise from the lack of economic prospects can fuel social movements and political ideologies that challenge the existing order. Addressing income inequality and wealth disparity is not only a matter of economic justice but also crucial for maintaining social stability and harmony.

Addressing the Divide

To mitigate income inequality and wealth disparity in a jobless society, it is imperative to implement policies and initiatives that promote economic inclusivity and equal opportunities. This requires a multi-faceted approach that includes:

1. Education and Skills Development

Investing in education and skills development is crucial to equip individuals with the tools they need to thrive in a changing job market. By providing accessible and quality education, vocational training, and lifelong learning opportunities, individuals can acquire the skills necessary to adapt to technological advancements and secure meaningful employment.

2. Progressive Taxation and Redistribution

Implementing progressive taxation policies can help redistribute wealth and reduce income inequality. By taxing the wealthy at higher rates and using those funds to invest in social welfare programs, governments can provide a safety net for those who are most vulnerable in a jobless society.

3. Universal Basic Income

Universal Basic Income (UBI) has gained traction as a potential solution to income inequality. UBI would provide a guaranteed income to all citizens, regardless of employment status, ensuring a basic standard of living for everyone. This approach aims to alleviate poverty, reduce income disparities, and provide individuals with the means to pursue education, entrepreneurship, or other endeavors.

4. Strengthening Labor Rights

Protecting and strengthening labor rights is essential to ensure fair wages, safe working conditions, and job security. By empowering workers and promoting collective bargaining, governments can help bridge the income gap and create a more equitable society.

5. Promoting Entrepreneurship and Innovation

Encouraging entrepreneurship and innovation can create new avenues for wealth creation and economic mobility. By providing support and resources to aspiring entrepreneurs, governments can foster a culture of innovation and empower individuals to create their own opportunities in a jobless society.

Conclusion

Income inequality and wealth disparity are significant challenges that arise in a jobless society. The concentration of wealth, disruption of traditional industries, and limited social mobility all contribute to the widening gap between the rich and the poor. However, by implementing comprehensive policies that prioritize education, progressive taxation, social welfare, and entrepreneurship, it is possible to address these issues and create a more equitable and inclusive future for all.

3.3 Social Implications of Joblessness

As we delve deeper into the jobless era, it is crucial to understand the social implications that arise from widespread unemployment. The absence of traditional employment opportunities has far-reaching consequences that extend beyond the individual level and impact society as a whole. In this section, we will explore the various social implications of joblessness and the challenges they present.

3.3.1 Loss of Identity and Self-Worth

For many individuals, their job plays a significant role in shaping their identity and providing a sense of purpose and self-worth. When jobs become scarce, people may experience a profound loss of identity, leading to feelings of worthlessness and despair. The absence of meaningful work can erode self-esteem and contribute to mental health issues such as depression and anxiety. As society transitions into a jobless era, it becomes crucial to address these psychological challenges and find alternative ways for individuals to derive a sense of purpose and fulfillment.

3.3.2 Increased Social Inequality

Joblessness exacerbates existing social inequalities and creates new ones. Without access to stable employment, individuals and families may struggle to meet their basic needs, leading to increased poverty and economic disparity. The gap between the rich and the poor widens as those with access to resources and opportunities continue to thrive while others are left behind. This growing inequality can lead to social unrest, resentment, and a breakdown of social cohesion. It is imperative for society to address these disparities and work towards creating a more equitable future.

3.3.3 Strained Social Safety Nets

In a jobless society, the demand for social safety nets and welfare programs increases significantly. As unemployment rises, governments must adapt and expand their social support systems to provide for those who are unable to find work. This places a strain on public resources and requires innovative solutions to ensure that everyone has access to basic necessities such as food, shelter, and healthcare. It is essential for governments to proactively address these challenges and develop sustainable social safety nets that can support individuals and families during periods of joblessness.

3.3.4 Disruption of Social Structures

Traditional social structures and institutions are deeply intertwined with the concept of work. As joblessness becomes more prevalent, these structures may undergo significant disruption. Communities that were once centered around industries and workplaces may struggle to adapt to the changing landscape. The loss of jobs can lead to the decline of local economies, increased migration, and the disintegration of social bonds. It is crucial for communities to come together and find new ways to foster social connections and support networks in the absence of traditional employment opportunities.

3.3.5 Impact on Education and Skills Development

The jobless era necessitates a reimagining of education and skills development. As traditional jobs become obsolete, individuals must acquire new skills to remain relevant in the changing job market. However, the lack of employment opportunities can make it challenging for individuals to invest in education and training. This creates a vicious cycle where joblessness hinders skills development, further perpetuating unemployment. It is essential for educational institutions and governments to collaborate and provide accessible and affordable opportunities for individuals to upskill and reskill, ensuring that they can adapt to the evolving job landscape.

3.3.6 Potential for Social Innovation

While joblessness presents numerous challenges, it also offers opportunities for social innovation. As traditional employment structures crumble, individuals and communities have the chance to explore alternative models of work and social organization. The jobless era can foster creativity and entrepreneurship, leading to the emergence of new industries and ways of living. By embracing this potential for innovation, society can harness the power of human ingenuity to create a more sustainable and inclusive future.

In conclusion, the social implications of joblessness are vast and multifaceted. From the loss of identity and self-worth to increased social inequality and strained social safety nets, the challenges are significant. However, by addressing these implications head-on and fostering social innovation, we can navigate the jobless era and create a future that prioritizes the well-being and fulfillment of all individuals.

3.4 The Role of Government in a Jobless Era

As the world transitions into a jobless era, the role of government becomes crucial in ensuring the well-being and stability of society. With automation and technological advancements replacing human labor at an unprecedented rate, governments must adapt and implement policies that address the challenges and opportunities presented by this new reality. In this section, we will explore the role of government in a jobless era and the various strategies they can employ to navigate this transformative period.

3.4.1 Redefining the Social Contract

The advent of automation and the subsequent rise in joblessness necessitates a reevaluation of the social contract between citizens and the government. Traditionally, the social contract has been based on the premise that individuals contribute to society through their labor in exchange for economic security and social benefits. However, in a jobless era, where traditional employment is scarce, this contract must be redefined to ensure that all members of society have access to a decent standard of living.

Governments can play a pivotal role in redefining the social contract by implementing policies such as universal basic income (UBI). UBI is a system in which every citizen receives a regular, unconditional cash payment from the government, regardless of their employment status. This approach provides a safety net for individuals who are unable to find traditional employment and helps to alleviate poverty and inequality.

3.4.2 Facilitating Transition and Reskilling

In a jobless era, it is essential for governments to facilitate the transition of workers into new industries and provide opportunities for reskilling and upskilling. This can be achieved through the establishment of comprehensive retraining programs and educational initiatives that equip individuals with the skills needed for the jobs of the future.

Governments can collaborate with educational institutions, industry leaders, and technology experts to identify emerging sectors and develop training programs tailored to the needs of these industries. By investing in lifelong learning and providing accessible education and training opportunities, governments can empower individuals to adapt to technological advancements and secure employment in new fields.

3.4.3 Fostering Innovation and Entrepreneurship

In a jobless era, governments must foster an environment that encourages innovation and entrepreneurship. By supporting startups and small businesses, governments can create new avenues for job creation and economic growth. This can be achieved through the provision of financial incentives, access to resources and infrastructure, and streamlined regulatory frameworks.

Furthermore, governments can invest in research and development to drive technological innovation and create new industries. By supporting scientific research and collaboration between academia and industry, governments can pave the way for the development of groundbreaking technologies that can generate employment opportunities.

3.4.4 Ensuring Social Safety Nets

As the nature of work changes, governments must ensure the existence of robust social safety nets to protect vulnerable individuals and communities. This includes comprehensive healthcare systems, affordable housing initiatives, and access to essential services such as education and childcare.

Additionally, governments can explore alternative models of employment and social protection, such as portable benefits, which provide workers with access to benefits regardless of their employment status or the specific job they perform. By adapting social safety nets to the realities of a jobless era, governments can mitigate the negative consequences of unemployment and income inequality.

3.4.5 Collaborating on a Global Scale

The challenges posed by a jobless era are not confined to individual nations but are global in nature. Governments must recognize the need for international collaboration and cooperation to address the complex issues arising from automation and joblessness.

By collaborating with other countries, governments can share best practices, exchange knowledge, and develop joint initiatives to tackle the challenges of a jobless era. This can include the establishment of international forums and organizations dedicated to addressing the social, economic, and ethical implications of automation and joblessness.

● ● ●

3.4.6 Ethical Considerations and Regulation

In a jobless era, governments must also address the ethical considerations surrounding automation and artificial intelligence. They must ensure that technological advancements are deployed in a manner that is fair, equitable, and respects human rights. This includes regulating the use of AI algorithms to prevent bias and discrimination, protecting privacy rights, and establishing guidelines for the ethical development and deployment of automation technologies.

Governments can work in collaboration with experts, industry leaders, and civil society organizations to develop comprehensive regulatory frameworks that safeguard the interests of individuals and society as a whole. By actively engaging in ethical considerations and regulation, governments can shape the future of work in a way that upholds human dignity and promotes social justice.

In conclusion, the role of government in a jobless era is multifaceted and crucial for ensuring the well-being and stability of society. By redefining the social contract, facilitating transition and reskilling, fostering innovation and entrepreneurship, ensuring social safety nets, collaborating on a global scale, and addressing ethical considerations, governments can navigate the challenges and opportunities presented by automation and joblessness. It is through proactive and forward-thinking policies that governments can create a positive future for all in the jobless era.

3.5 Universal Basic Income

In a world where automation and technological advancements have rendered many jobs obsolete, the concept of Universal Basic Income (UBI) has gained significant attention and debate. UBI is a system in which every citizen of a country receives a regular, unconditional sum of money from the government, regardless of their employment status. It is seen as a potential solution to address the challenges posed by widespread joblessness and income inequality in a jobless era.

The Concept of Universal Basic Income

The idea of providing a basic income to all citizens is not a new one. It has been discussed and experimented with in various forms throughout history. However, the rise of automation and the potential for widespread job displacement has brought the concept of UBI to the forefront of public discourse.

The fundamental principle behind UBI is to ensure that every individual has access to a minimum level of income to meet their basic needs, such as food, shelter, and healthcare. By providing a guaranteed income, UBI aims to alleviate poverty, reduce income inequality, and provide individuals with the freedom to pursue their interests and passions, even if traditional employment opportunities are limited.

Proponents of UBI argue that it has several potential benefits in a jobless society. Firstly, it can act as a safety net, providing financial security to individuals who have lost their jobs due to automation or other economic shifts. This can help prevent extreme poverty and social unrest that may arise from widespread unemployment.

Secondly, UBI has the potential to stimulate economic growth. By providing a basic income to all citizens, it ensures that money flows into the hands of consumers, increasing their purchasing power. This, in turn, can drive demand for goods and services, leading to increased economic activity and job creation in new sectors.

Furthermore, UBI can foster innovation and entrepreneurship. With a guaranteed income, individuals have the freedom to take risks and pursue entrepreneurial ventures without the fear of financial ruin. This can lead to the creation of new businesses, products, and services, contributing to economic development and societal progress.

Criticisms and Challenges of Universal Basic Income

While UBI has its proponents, it also faces criticism and challenges. One of the main concerns is the potential cost of implementing such a program. Critics argue that providing a basic income to all citizens would require a significant amount of government funding, which may lead to increased taxes or unsustainable levels of public debt.

• • •

Another criticism is the potential disincentive to work. Skeptics argue that if individuals receive a guaranteed income without the need to work, it may discourage them from seeking employment or pursuing higher education. This could lead to a decline in productivity and a lack of skilled workers in essential sectors.

Additionally, there are concerns about the potential impact of UBI on inflation. If everyone has more money to spend, it could drive up prices, making goods and services more expensive and potentially eroding the purchasing power of the basic income.

Pilot Programs and Experiments

To explore the feasibility and potential impact of UBI, several pilot programs and experiments have been conducted around the world. These initiatives aim to gather data and insights into the effects of providing a basic income to individuals.

For example, in Finland, a two-year experiment was conducted from 2017 to 2018, where a group of unemployed individuals received a monthly basic income. The results showed that while the participants experienced improved well-being and reduced stress, there was no significant increase in employment rates.

Similarly, in Canada, the province of Ontario launched a basic income pilot project in 2017. However, the program was abruptly canceled after a change in government, preventing a comprehensive evaluation of its impact.

These pilot programs provide valuable insights into the potential benefits and challenges of implementing UBI on a larger scale. They also highlight the need for careful planning, evaluation, and adaptation of UBI policies to ensure their effectiveness.

The Future of Universal Basic Income

As the job market continues to evolve and automation becomes more prevalent, the discussion around UBI is likely to intensify. The concept of providing a basic income to all citizens has both enthusiastic supporters and staunch critics.

To successfully implement UBI, policymakers must address the challenges and concerns associated with the program. This includes determining the appropriate funding mechanisms, designing effective implementation strategies, and considering the potential impact on the labor market and economy as a whole.

Moreover, the future of UBI should be seen as part of a broader conversation about the role of work, the distribution of wealth, and the social contract in a jobless era. It requires a comprehensive examination of the societal implications of joblessness and the need for alternative systems to ensure the well-being and dignity of all individuals.

In conclusion, Universal Basic Income is a concept that holds promise in addressing the challenges posed by widespread joblessness in a rapidly changing world. While it has its critics and challenges, UBI has the potential to provide financial security, stimulate economic growth, and foster innovation. As we navigate the complexities of a jobless society, the exploration and experimentation with UBI will continue to shape the future of work and social welfare.

3.6 Reimagining Education and Training

In a jobless era, where automation and technology have replaced many traditional jobs, the need for reimagining education and training becomes paramount. As the nature of work continues to evolve, it is crucial for individuals and societies to adapt and equip themselves with the necessary skills to thrive in this new landscape.

3.6.1 The Changing Role of Education

Traditional education systems have primarily focused on preparing individuals for specific careers and professions. However, in a jobless society, where job roles are constantly shifting or disappearing altogether, a new approach to education is required. Education needs to shift from a focus on rote memorization and standardized testing to a more holistic and adaptable model.

3.6.2 Emphasizing Critical Thinking and Problem-Solving Skills

One of the key skills that individuals will need in a jobless era is the ability to think critically and solve complex problems. With automation taking over routine tasks, humans will need to focus on tasks that require creativity, innovation, and problem-solving abilities. Education systems should prioritize the development of these skills through project-based learning, collaborative problem-solving, and real-world applications.

3.6.3 Cultivating Creativity and Innovation

Creativity and innovation will be highly valued in a jobless society. These skills enable individuals to come up with new ideas, think outside the box, and find unique solutions to challenges. Education should foster creativity by encouraging curiosity, exploration, and experimentation. Arts, music, and other creative disciplines should be integrated into the curriculum to nurture the imagination and encourage innovative thinking.

3.6.4 Developing Digital Literacy and Technological Skills

As technology continues to advance, digital literacy and technological skills will become essential for individuals to navigate the job market. Education systems should prioritize teaching digital literacy, coding, data analysis, and other relevant technological skills. By equipping individuals with these skills, they will be better prepared to adapt to technological changes and leverage technology to their advantage.

3.6.5 Lifelong Learning and Continuous Skill Development

In a jobless era, learning should not be confined to the early years of life or limited to formal education institutions. Lifelong learning and continuous skill development will be crucial for individuals to remain relevant and adaptable in the changing job market. Education systems should promote a culture of lifelong learning, providing opportunities for individuals to upskill and reskill throughout their lives.

3.6.6 Embracing Interdisciplinary Education

The jobless era calls for a more interdisciplinary approach to education. Traditional silos between subjects should be broken down to encourage cross-disciplinary learning. By integrating different fields of study, individuals can develop a broader understanding of complex issues and gain a diverse skill set that can be applied to a variety of roles. Interdisciplinary education fosters adaptability and prepares individuals for the multidimensional challenges of the future.

3.6.7 Entrepreneurship and Innovation Education

With traditional employment opportunities becoming scarcer, entrepreneurship and innovation will play a significant role in the jobless era. Education systems should incorporate entrepreneurship education, teaching individuals how to identify opportunities, develop business plans, and navigate the challenges of starting and running a business. By fostering an entrepreneurial mindset, individuals can create their own opportunities and contribute to economic growth.

3.6.8 Collaboration and Communication Skills

In a jobless society, collaboration and communication skills will be highly valued. As humans continue to work alongside machines, the ability to effectively collaborate with others and communicate ideas will become essential. Education systems should emphasize teamwork, communication, and interpersonal skills, enabling individuals to work effectively in diverse teams and adapt to changing work dynamics.

3.6.9 Personal Development and Emotional Intelligence

In a world where human connection and empathy are increasingly important, education should focus on personal development and emotional intelligence. Individuals should be encouraged to develop self-awareness, empathy, and resilience. Education systems should incorporate social and emotional learning, teaching individuals how to manage their emotions, build positive relationships, and navigate the complexities of human interaction.

3.6.10 Adapting Education to Technological Advances

As technology continues to advance, education systems must adapt to incorporate emerging technologies. Virtual reality, augmented reality, artificial intelligence, and other technologies can enhance the learning experience and provide individuals with immersive and interactive educational opportunities. By embracing these technologies, education can become more engaging, personalized, and effective.

In a jobless era, education and training must evolve to meet the changing needs of individuals and society. By reimagining education, emphasizing critical thinking, creativity, digital literacy, and lifelong learning, individuals can equip themselves with the skills necessary to thrive in a jobless society. Collaboration, entrepreneurship, and emotional intelligence will also play crucial roles in this new era. As technology continues to advance, education must adapt and incorporate emerging technologies to provide individuals with the best possible learning experience. By embracing these changes, we can create a future where individuals are empowered to navigate the jobless era with confidence and resilience.

4

The Human Element

4.1 The Importance of Human Skills

In a world where automation and technology are rapidly advancing, the importance of human skills cannot be overstated. While machines and algorithms can perform many tasks more efficiently and accurately than humans, there are certain skills that are uniquely human and cannot be replicated by technology alone. These skills are not only valuable in the job market but also crucial for our personal and societal well-being.

4.1.1 Emotional Intelligence and Empathy

One of the most significant human skills that sets us apart from machines is emotional intelligence and empathy. These skills allow us to understand and connect with others on a deeper level, to recognize and manage our own emotions, and to navigate complex social situations. In a jobless era, where human interaction may become increasingly limited, the ability to empathize and understand the emotions of others will become even more valuable.

Emotional intelligence enables us to build strong relationships, resolve conflicts, and collaborate effectively. It allows us to provide emotional support and comfort to those in need, making us indispensable in roles that require human connection and care. Whether it's in healthcare, counseling, customer service, or leadership positions, the ability to understand and respond to the emotions of others will be highly sought after.

4.1.2 Creativity and Innovation in a Jobless Era

Creativity and innovation are fundamental human skills that drive progress and advancement. While machines can analyze data and perform routine tasks, they lack the ability to think outside the box, imagine new possibilities, and come up with innovative solutions to complex problems. In a jobless era, where automation takes over repetitive and predictable tasks, creativity becomes a valuable asset.

Creative thinking allows us to generate new ideas, adapt to changing circumstances, and find novel approaches to challenges. It enables us to envision alternative futures and explore uncharted territories. Whether it's in the fields of art, design, entrepreneurship, or scientific research, the ability to think creatively will be in high demand. Embracing our creative potential will not only help us thrive in a jobless society but also contribute to the advancement of humanity as a whole.

4.1.3 Critical Thinking and Problem-Solving

Critical thinking and problem-solving skills are essential for navigating the complexities of the modern world. While machines can process vast amounts of information, humans possess the ability to analyze, evaluate, and interpret that information in a meaningful way. Critical thinking allows us to question assumptions, identify biases, and make informed decisions.

In a jobless era, where the nature of work is constantly evolving, the ability to think critically and adapt to new situations becomes crucial. These skills enable us to identify problems, analyze their root causes, and develop effective solutions. Whether it's in the fields of management, research, policy-making, or entrepreneurship, the ability to think critically and solve complex problems will be highly valued.

4.1.4 Communication and Collaboration

Effective communication and collaboration are vital skills that facilitate teamwork, cooperation, and the exchange of ideas. While machines can transmit information quickly, humans possess the ability to convey meaning, build relationships, and inspire others through verbal and nonverbal communication.

In a jobless era, where remote work and virtual collaboration may become the norm, the ability to communicate effectively across different mediums and cultures becomes even more important. These skills enable us to build trust, resolve conflicts, and foster a

● ● ●

sense of belonging within teams and communities. Whether it's in the fields of project management, sales, teaching, or community organizing, the ability to communicate and collaborate will be essential for success.

4.1.5 Adaptability and Lifelong Learning

In a rapidly changing job market, adaptability and lifelong learning are critical skills for staying relevant and thriving. As technology continues to advance, new jobs will emerge, and existing jobs will evolve. The ability to adapt to new technologies, learn new skills, and embrace change will be essential for navigating the jobless era.

Adaptable individuals are open to new ideas, flexible in their thinking, and willing to step out of their comfort zones. They embrace challenges as opportunities for growth and continuously seek to expand their knowledge and skills. Whether it's through formal education, online courses, or self-directed learning, the commitment to lifelong learning will be a key factor in remaining employable and resilient in the face of technological disruption.

Conclusion

While the rise of automation and the jobless era may bring significant changes to the world of work, the importance of human skills cannot be underestimated. Emotional intelligence, creativity, critical thinking, communication, and adaptability are just a few examples of the skills that make us uniquely human.

● ● ●

These skills not only provide value in the job market but also contribute to our personal fulfillment and the well-being of society as a whole. As we navigate the future, it is crucial to recognize and nurture these skills to ensure a positive and prosperous jobless era.

4.2 Creativity and Innovation in a Jobless Era

In a jobless era where automation and technology have taken over many traditional jobs, creativity and innovation become crucial for individuals and society as a whole. As the demand for routine and repetitive tasks decreases, the value of human creativity and the ability to think outside the box increases exponentially. This chapter explores the importance of creativity and innovation in a jobless era and how individuals can harness these skills to thrive in the changing landscape of work.

The Power of Creativity

Creativity is the ability to generate new ideas, concepts, and solutions. It is a uniquely human trait that sets us apart from machines. In a jobless era, where routine tasks are automated, creativity becomes a highly sought-after skill. It allows individuals to adapt, create, and innovate in ways that machines cannot replicate.

Creativity is not limited to artistic endeavors; it extends to problem-solving, critical thinking, and finding new approaches to challenges. It enables individuals to identify opportunities, envision possibilities, and develop unique solutions to complex problems. In a world where jobs are scarce, those who can think creatively have a distinct advantage.

Fostering Innovation

Innovation is the process of turning creative ideas into practical solutions that create value. It involves taking risks, challenging the status quo, and implementing new approaches. In a jobless era, innovation becomes essential for individuals and organizations to remain relevant and competitive.

To foster innovation, individuals must cultivate a mindset that embraces change and encourages experimentation. They must be willing to take calculated risks, learn from failures, and continuously adapt. Organizations can create an environment that nurtures innovation by promoting a culture of openness, collaboration, and learning. By encouraging employees to think creatively and providing them with the resources and support to explore new ideas, organizations can drive innovation and stay ahead of the curve.

The Role of Creativity and Innovation in Job Creation

While automation and technology may eliminate certain jobs, they also create new opportunities. Creativity and innovation play a vital role in identifying and capitalizing on these emerging job prospects. As industries evolve and new technologies emerge, individuals who can think creatively and adapt quickly will be in high demand.

● ● ●

Creativity and innovation can lead to the development of new products, services, and industries. They can also drive entrepreneurship and the creation of new businesses. By embracing these skills, individuals can carve out their own paths and create meaningful work opportunities in a jobless era.

Nurturing Creativity and Innovation

To thrive in a jobless era, individuals must actively nurture their creativity and innovation skills. Here are some strategies to cultivate these abilities:

4.2.1 Embrace Curiosity and Lifelong Learning

Curiosity is the fuel for creativity and innovation. By cultivating a sense of curiosity, individuals can explore new ideas, ask questions, and seek out diverse perspectives. Lifelong learning is also crucial in a rapidly changing world. By continuously acquiring new knowledge and skills, individuals can stay ahead of the curve and adapt to emerging trends and technologies.

4.2.2 Foster a Creative Environment

Creating an environment that fosters creativity is essential. This can be achieved by surrounding oneself with diverse perspectives, engaging in brainstorming sessions, and encouraging open dialogue. Taking breaks, engaging in hobbies, and exposing oneself to different experiences can also stimulate creativity.

4.2.3 Embrace Failure and Learn from Mistakes

Failure is an inevitable part of the creative process. Embracing failure as a learning opportunity allows individuals to take risks and push boundaries. By analyzing failures and learning from mistakes, individuals can refine their ideas and improve their creative output.

4.2.4 Collaborate and Seek Feedback

Collaboration and feedback are invaluable in the creative process. By working with others, individuals can benefit from different perspectives, ideas, and expertise. Seeking feedback from peers, mentors, and experts can provide valuable insights and help refine creative ideas.

4.2.5 Practice Divergent Thinking

Divergent thinking is the ability to generate multiple solutions to a problem. By practicing divergent thinking, individuals can expand their creative capacity and explore a wide range of possibilities. Techniques such as brainstorming, mind mapping, and free writing can help stimulate divergent thinking.

Conclusion

In a jobless era, creativity and innovation become essential skills for individuals and society. They enable individuals to adapt, create new opportunities, and drive economic growth. By nurturing creativity, embracing innovation, and continuously developing these skills, individuals can thrive in a changing job market and contribute to a future where human ingenuity remains invaluable.

4.3 Emotional Intelligence and Empathy

In a jobless era, where automation and technology have taken over many traditional job roles, the importance of emotional intelligence and empathy cannot be overstated. As machines become more proficient at performing tasks that were once exclusive to humans, it is the uniquely human qualities of emotional intelligence and empathy that will set us apart and become even more valuable.

The Role of Emotional Intelligence

Emotional intelligence refers to the ability to recognize, understand, and manage our own emotions, as well as the emotions of others. It encompasses skills such as self-awareness, self-regulation, empathy, and social skills. These skills are crucial in navigating the complexities of human interactions and building meaningful relationships.

In a jobless era, where human connection and interaction may become scarce, emotional intelligence becomes even more essential. As people face the challenges of unemployment and the uncertainty of the future, those with high emotional intelligence will be better equipped to handle the emotional rollercoaster and support others in similar situations.

● ● ●

Empathy, closely related to emotional intelligence, is the ability to understand and share the feelings of others. It involves putting oneself in someone else's shoes and experiencing their emotions. Empathy allows us to connect with others on a deeper level, fostering understanding, compassion, and support.

In a society where joblessness is prevalent, empathy becomes a vital tool for building a sense of community and solidarity. It enables individuals to offer support and comfort to those who are struggling, creating a network of understanding and compassion. Empathy helps to alleviate the feelings of isolation and despair that can arise from unemployment, providing a sense of belonging and hope.

The Benefits of Emotional Intelligence and Empathy

Emotional intelligence and empathy offer numerous benefits in a jobless era. Here are a few ways in which these qualities can positively impact individuals and society as a whole:

1. Mental Well-being

Unemployment can take a toll on mental health, leading to feelings of anxiety, depression, and low self-esteem. Emotional intelligence and empathy can help individuals navigate these challenges by providing them with the tools to manage their emotions effectively and seek support from others. By understanding and empathizing with their own feelings and those of others, individuals can develop resilience and maintain a positive mindset.

2. Building Stronger Relationships

In a world where face-to-face interactions may become less frequent, the ability to connect with others on an emotional level becomes even more crucial. Emotional intelligence and empathy allow individuals to build stronger and more meaningful relationships, both personally and professionally. By understanding the emotions and needs of others, individuals can foster trust, collaboration, and mutual support.

3. Effective Communication

Clear and effective communication is essential in any situation, but it becomes even more critical in a jobless era. Emotional intelligence enables individuals to express their thoughts and feelings in a way that is empathetic and understanding. By being attuned to the emotions of others, individuals can communicate with empathy and compassion, fostering positive and productive conversations.

4. Problem-solving and Conflict Resolution

Emotional intelligence and empathy play a significant role in problem-solving and conflict resolution. By understanding the emotions and perspectives of others, individuals can approach conflicts with empathy and find mutually beneficial solutions. These qualities also enable individuals to navigate complex situations and make informed decisions, taking into account the emotions and needs of all parties involved.

5. Leadership and Teamwork

In a jobless era, leadership and teamwork skills become even more valuable. Emotional intelligence and empathy are essential qualities for effective leadership and collaboration. Leaders who possess these qualities can inspire and motivate their teams, creating a positive and supportive work environment. Empathy allows leaders to understand the challenges faced by their team members and provide the necessary support and guidance.

Cultivating Emotional Intelligence and Empathy

While some individuals may naturally possess higher levels of emotional intelligence and empathy, these qualities can also be developed and nurtured. Here are a few strategies to cultivate emotional intelligence and empathy in a jobless era:

1. Self-reflection and Self-awareness

Developing emotional intelligence starts with self-reflection and self-awareness. Take the time to understand your own emotions, strengths, and weaknesses. Reflect on how your emotions impact your thoughts and actions. By becoming more self-aware, you can better understand and manage your emotions, leading to improved empathy towards others.

2. Active Listening

Active listening is a crucial skill for developing empathy. Practice truly listening to others without judgment or interruption. Pay attention to their verbal and non-verbal cues, and try to understand their emotions and perspectives. By actively listening, you can foster deeper connections and demonstrate empathy towards others.

3. Practice Perspective-taking

Perspective-taking involves putting yourself in someone else's shoes and seeing the world from their point of view. This practice helps to develop empathy by allowing you to understand and appreciate the emotions and experiences of others. Engage in conversations with people from diverse backgrounds and actively seek to understand their perspectives.

4. Seek Opportunities for Emotional Growth

Look for opportunities to enhance your emotional intelligence and empathy. Engage in activities that challenge you to manage your emotions effectively, such as volunteering or participating in group discussions. Seek feedback from others to gain insights into how your emotions and actions impact those around you.

5. Continuous Learning and Development

Emotional intelligence and empathy are skills that can be continually developed and refined. Stay open to learning and seek out resources, such as books,

●●●

workshops, or online courses, that can help you deepen your understanding of these qualities. Surround yourself with individuals who possess high emotional intelligence and learn from their example.

In a jobless era, where the human element becomes increasingly valuable, emotional intelligence and empathy are the qualities that will set individuals apart. By cultivating these skills, individuals can navigate the challenges of unemployment, build stronger relationships, and contribute to a more compassionate and supportive society.

4.4 The Value of Human Connection

In a world where automation and technology are rapidly replacing human labor, it is easy to overlook the importance of human connection. As we navigate through the jobless era, it becomes crucial to recognize and appreciate the value that human interaction brings to our lives. While machines can perform tasks efficiently and accurately, they lack the emotional intelligence, empathy, and creativity that only humans possess.

4.4.1 The Power of Emotional Connection

One of the most significant aspects of human connection is the power of emotional bonding. Humans are social beings, and we thrive on meaningful relationships and connections with others. These connections provide us with a sense of belonging, support, and understanding. In a jobless society, where many individuals may find themselves isolated due to lack of employment, the importance of emotional connection becomes even more pronounced.

Emotional connection allows us to share our joys, sorrows, and experiences with others. It provides a support system that can help us navigate through challenging times and find solace in the company of others. Whether it is a close friend, a family member, or a partner, these connections offer a sense of purpose and fulfillment that cannot be replicated by machines.

4.4.2 Fostering Creativity and Innovation

Human connection is also essential for fostering creativity and innovation. When individuals come together, they bring with them unique perspectives, ideas, and experiences. Through collaboration and interaction, these diverse viewpoints can merge, leading to the generation of new and innovative solutions to complex problems.

In a jobless era, where the demand for creative thinking and problem-solving skills is higher than ever, human connection becomes a catalyst for innovation. By engaging in discussions, brainstorming sessions, and collaborative projects, individuals can tap into their collective intelligence and create groundbreaking ideas that can shape the future.

4.4.3 Empathy and Understanding

Empathy, the ability to understand and share the feelings of others, is a fundamental aspect of human connection. It allows us to put ourselves in someone else's shoes, to truly comprehend their experiences, and to offer support and compassion. Empathy is a uniquely human trait that cannot be replicated by machines.

In a jobless society, where individuals may face financial hardships, emotional distress, or feelings of worthlessness, empathy becomes a lifeline. It helps create a sense of community and solidarity, reminding individuals that they are not alone in their struggles. Through empathy, we can provide comfort, encouragement, and assistance to those in need, fostering a society that values human connection and supports one another.

4.4.4 The Role of Human Connection in the Workplace

While automation and technology may replace many jobs, there are certain roles that require the human touch. Industries such as healthcare, counseling, teaching, and customer service rely heavily on human connection to provide effective and meaningful services.

In healthcare, for example, the role of doctors, nurses, and other healthcare professionals goes beyond diagnosing and treating patients. It involves building trust, providing emotional support, and offering personalized care. Similarly, in customer service, the ability to empathize, understand customer needs, and provide a human touch is crucial for building strong customer relationships.

4.4.5 Nurturing Relationships in a Digital Age

In a world dominated by technology and digital communication, it is essential to find ways to nurture and maintain meaningful relationships. While social media and online platforms offer opportunities for connection, they can also lead to superficial interactions and a sense of isolation.

To truly value human connection, we must prioritize face-to-face interactions, engage in active listening, and invest time and effort in building and maintaining relationships. This may involve organizing social gatherings, participating in community events, or simply reaching out to friends and loved ones for a heartfelt conversation.

4.4.6 The Future of Human Connection

As we move forward into the jobless era, it is crucial to recognize the value of human connection and actively cultivate it in our lives. While technology and automation may continue to advance, the need for human interaction, empathy, and creativity will remain essential.

In a society where jobs may be scarce, human connection can provide a sense of purpose, fulfillment, and support. By embracing the power of emotional connection, fostering creativity and innovation, and nurturing relationships, we can create a future that values the unique qualities that only humans possess.

The jobless era presents us with an opportunity to redefine the way we view work and the role of human connection in our lives. By embracing the value of human connection, we can build a society that prioritizes the well-being and fulfillment of its members, creating a future that is not only technologically advanced but also deeply human.

5

Preparing for the Future

5.1 Adapting to Technological Change

As we navigate the ever-evolving landscape of the job market, it is crucial to understand the importance of adapting to technological change. The rapid advancements in technology, particularly in automation and artificial intelligence, have revolutionized the way we work. To thrive in this new era, individuals must be proactive in upskilling and reskilling themselves to remain relevant and competitive.

5.1.1 The Need for Continuous Learning

In a world where technology is constantly evolving, the ability to learn and adapt becomes paramount. Traditional job roles are being replaced by automated systems, and new jobs are emerging that require a different set of skills. To stay ahead of the curve, individuals must embrace lifelong learning.

Continuous learning involves acquiring new knowledge, skills, and competencies throughout one's career. It is no longer sufficient to rely solely on the education and training received in the past. Instead, individuals must actively seek out opportunities to expand their skill sets and stay updated with the latest technological advancements.

5.1.2 Embracing Upskilling and Reskilling

Upskilling and reskilling are essential strategies for adapting to technological change. Upskilling refers to the process of acquiring new skills or enhancing existing ones to perform better in one's current job or to prepare for future roles. Reskilling, on the other hand, involves learning entirely new skills to transition into a different field or occupation.

To identify the skills that are in demand, individuals should stay informed about industry trends and job market forecasts. This knowledge will help them make informed decisions about which skills to prioritize in their upskilling or reskilling efforts. Additionally, seeking guidance from career counselors or industry professionals can provide valuable insights into the skills that are most relevant and sought after.

Online learning platforms, vocational training programs, and professional development courses are excellent resources for acquiring new skills. These platforms offer a wide range of courses that cater to various industries and skill levels. By taking advantage of these opportunities, individuals can enhance their employability and adaptability in the face of technological change.

5.1.3 The Role of Entrepreneurship and Self-Employment

As traditional job roles become obsolete, entrepreneurship and self-employment offer alternative paths for individuals to navigate the changing job market. Embracing an entrepreneurial mindset allows individuals to create their own opportunities and take control of their careers.

Starting a business or becoming self-employed requires a combination of skills, including creativity, problem-solving, and adaptability. Entrepreneurs must be willing to take risks, learn from failures, and continuously innovate to stay competitive. By leveraging technology and identifying gaps in the market, individuals can carve out their own niche and thrive in a jobless era.

Furthermore, self-employment provides individuals with the flexibility to adapt to technological change. They can quickly pivot their business models, explore new markets, and embrace emerging technologies without the constraints of traditional employment structures. This adaptability is crucial in a rapidly evolving technological landscape.

5.1.4 Building Resilience in a Changing Job Market

Adapting to technological change requires resilience and a proactive mindset. The job market will continue to evolve, and individuals must be prepared to face uncertainties and challenges. Building resilience involves developing the ability to bounce back from setbacks, embrace change, and remain optimistic about future opportunities.

One way to build resilience is by diversifying skills and knowledge. Instead of relying on a single skill set, individuals should aim to develop a broad range of competencies that can be applied across different industries. This versatility allows individuals to adapt to changing job requirements and explore new career paths.

Networking and building professional relationships are also crucial in a changing job market. By connecting with like-minded individuals, industry professionals, and mentors, individuals can gain valuable insights, access new opportunities, and stay updated with industry trends. Networking can also provide a support system during times of uncertainty and serve as a platform for collaboration and knowledge sharing.

In conclusion, adapting to technological change is essential for thriving in a jobless era. Continuous learning, upskilling, and reskilling are crucial strategies for remaining relevant and competitive. Embracing entrepreneurship and self-employment can provide individuals with the flexibility to navigate the changing job market. Building resilience through diversifying skills and networking is vital for embracing the uncertainties of the future. By embracing these strategies, individuals can position themselves for success in the face of technological advancements.

5.2 Upskilling and Reskilling

In a rapidly changing job market, where automation and technology are replacing traditional jobs, it is crucial for individuals to adapt and acquire new skills to remain relevant and employable. Upskilling and reskilling have become essential strategies for navigating the jobless era and securing future employment opportunities.

5.2.1 The Need for Upskilling and Reskilling

As automation continues to advance, many jobs that were once performed by humans are now being taken over by machines. This shift in the job market requires individuals to develop new skills that are in demand and align with the evolving needs of industries. Upskilling refers to the process of acquiring additional skills or knowledge in one's current field, while reskilling involves learning new skills for a different occupation or industry.

The need for upskilling and reskilling arises from the fact that certain skills become obsolete or less valuable due to automation. Jobs that involve repetitive tasks or routine activities are particularly vulnerable to automation. However, automation also creates new opportunities and demands for skills that are uniquely human, such as critical thinking, problem-solving, creativity, and emotional intelligence.

5.2.2 Identifying In-Demand Skills

To effectively upskill or reskill, individuals must identify the skills that are in high demand in the job market. This requires staying informed about industry trends, technological advancements, and emerging job roles. Conducting research, attending industry conferences, and networking with professionals in the field can provide valuable insights into the skills that are sought after by employers.

Some of the skills that are expected to be in high demand in the jobless era include:

5.2.2.1 Digital Literacy and Technology Skills

As technology continues to shape the job market, digital literacy and technology skills have become essential for almost every occupation. Proficiency in using digital tools, software, and platforms is crucial for effective communication, data analysis, problem-solving, and collaboration. Skills such as coding, data analytics, cybersecurity, and artificial intelligence are particularly valuable in the digital age.

5.2.2.2 Critical Thinking and Problem-Solving

Automation may handle routine tasks, but it cannot replicate human creativity, critical thinking, and problem-solving abilities. These skills involve the ability to analyze complex situations, think critically, and develop innovative solutions. Employers value individuals who can approach challenges with a fresh perspective and find creative ways to overcome them.

5.2.2.3 Adaptability and Flexibility

In a rapidly changing job market, adaptability and flexibility are crucial skills. The ability to quickly learn

• • •

new skills, adapt to new technologies, and embrace change is highly valued by employers. Being open to new ideas, being willing to take on new responsibilities, and being able to work in diverse teams are all attributes that can enhance an individual's employability.

5.2.2.4 Emotional Intelligence and Interpersonal Skills

While automation may handle certain tasks, it cannot replace the human touch. Emotional intelligence, which includes self-awareness, empathy, and effective communication, is highly valued in the workplace. Interpersonal skills such as teamwork, leadership, and conflict resolution are also essential for building strong relationships and collaborating effectively with others.

5.2.3 Strategies for Upskilling and Reskilling

Once individuals have identified the skills they need to acquire, there are several strategies they can employ to upskill or reskill effectively:

5.2.3.1 Formal Education and Training

Formal education and training programs, such as university degrees, vocational courses, and certifications, can provide individuals with the necessary knowledge and skills to enter new fields or advance in their current careers. These programs offer structured learning opportunities and often provide hands-on experience and industry connections.

5.2.3.2 Online Learning Platforms

The rise of online learning platforms has made it easier than ever to access a wide range of courses and educational resources. Platforms such as Coursera, Udemy, and LinkedIn Learning offer courses on various topics, allowing individuals to learn at their own pace and from the comfort of their homes. Online learning provides flexibility and affordability, making it an attractive option for upskilling and reskilling.

5.2.3.3 Apprenticeships and Internships

Apprenticeships and internships provide individuals with the opportunity to gain practical experience and learn from industry professionals. These programs often combine on-the-job training with classroom instruction, allowing individuals to develop the skills needed for a specific occupation. Apprenticeships and internships can be particularly beneficial for those looking to switch careers or enter industries that require hands-on experience.

5.2.3.4 Professional Development and Networking

Engaging in professional development activities, such as attending workshops, conferences, and seminars, can help individuals stay updated on industry trends and expand their knowledge and skills. Networking with professionals in the field can also provide valuable insights and opportunities for growth. Building relationships with industry experts and mentors can open doors to new career prospects and help individuals navigate the job market effectively.

● ● ●

5.2.4 Benefits of Upskilling and Reskilling

Upskilling and reskilling offer numerous benefits for individuals in the jobless era:

5.2.4.1 Increased Employability

By acquiring new skills and staying relevant in the job market, individuals increase their employability and enhance their chances of securing employment. Upskilling and reskilling demonstrate a commitment to personal and professional growth, making individuals more attractive to employers.

5.2.4.2 Career Advancement

Upskilling and reskilling can open doors to new career opportunities and enable individuals to advance in their chosen fields. By acquiring in-demand skills, individuals position themselves for higher-paying roles and increased job satisfaction.

5.2.4.3 Adaptability to Technological Change

As technology continues to evolve, individuals who possess the skills needed to navigate and leverage new technologies will be better equipped to adapt to the changing job market. Upskilling and reskilling ensure that individuals can embrace technological advancements rather than being left behind.

5.2.4.4 Personal Growth and Fulfillment

Learning new skills and expanding one's knowledge can lead to personal growth and fulfillment. Upskilling and reskilling allow individuals to explore new interests, challenge themselves, and discover their potential in different areas.

In conclusion, upskilling and reskilling are essential strategies for individuals to thrive in the jobless era. By identifying in-demand skills, pursuing formal education or online learning, participating in apprenticeships or internships, and engaging in professional development and networking, individuals can enhance their employability, adapt to technological change, and unlock new career opportunities. Embracing lifelong learning and being proactive in acquiring new skills will be key to navigating the future of work successfully.

5.3 Entrepreneurship and Self-Employment

In a jobless era where traditional employment opportunities are scarce, entrepreneurship and self-employment become increasingly important. As automation and technology continue to reshape the job market, individuals must adapt and find new ways to create value and generate income. This chapter explores the role of entrepreneurship and self-employment in the future of work and provides insights into how individuals can navigate this changing landscape.

5.3.1 The Rise of Entrepreneurship

Entrepreneurship has always been a driving force behind economic growth and innovation. In a jobless era, it becomes even more crucial as individuals take charge of their own destinies and create their own opportunities. The rise of entrepreneurship offers a way for people to leverage their skills, knowledge, and creativity to build businesses and generate income.

One of the key advantages of entrepreneurship is the ability to adapt quickly to changing circumstances. In a rapidly evolving job market, entrepreneurs can identify emerging trends and capitalize on new opportunities. They have the flexibility to pivot their business models and offerings to meet the needs of the market. This adaptability is a valuable asset in a world where traditional jobs are disappearing.

5.3.2 The Benefits of Self-Employment

Self-employment provides individuals with a sense of autonomy and control over their work. Instead of relying on a single employer, self-employed individuals have the freedom to choose their clients, projects, and working hours. This flexibility allows them to create a work-life balance that suits their needs and preferences.

Moreover, self-employment offers the opportunity to pursue one's passions and interests. Many individuals find fulfillment in turning their hobbies or skills into profitable ventures. By doing what they love, self-employed individuals can find a sense of purpose and satisfaction in their work.

Another benefit of self-employment is the potential for higher income. While entrepreneurship comes with its own risks and challenges, successful self-employed individuals have the potential to earn more than they would in traditional employment. By building a strong brand, delivering high-quality products or services, and effectively marketing themselves, self-employed individuals can attract a loyal customer base and command higher prices.

5.3.3 Navigating the Challenges

While entrepreneurship and self-employment offer numerous benefits, they also come with challenges that individuals must navigate. One of the primary challenges is the uncertainty and risk associated with starting a business. Unlike traditional employment, where a steady paycheck is guaranteed, entrepreneurs and self-employed individuals must be prepared for fluctuations in income and the possibility of failure.

To mitigate these risks, it is essential for aspiring entrepreneurs to conduct thorough market research and develop a solid business plan. Understanding the target market, identifying competitors, and assessing the demand for their products or services can help individuals make informed decisions and increase their chances of success.

Another challenge is the need for a diverse skill set. As a self-employed individual, one must wear multiple hats and be proficient in various areas such as marketing, finance, customer service, and operations. Developing these skills or seeking assistance from professionals can help entrepreneurs effectively manage their businesses and overcome challenges.

5.3.4 Embracing Innovation and Technology

In a jobless era, embracing innovation and technology is crucial for entrepreneurs and self-employed individuals. Technology can be a powerful tool for streamlining operations, reaching a wider audience, and staying competitive in the market. From online platforms and e-commerce websites to social media marketing and automation tools, technology offers a range of opportunities for entrepreneurs to grow their businesses.

Furthermore, entrepreneurs should stay updated on emerging technologies and trends that can disrupt their industries. By embracing these innovations and incorporating them into their business strategies, entrepreneurs can stay ahead of the curve and continue to provide value to their customers.

5.3.5 Collaboration and Networking

In a jobless era, collaboration and networking become even more important for entrepreneurs and self-employed individuals. Building a strong network of like-minded individuals, industry experts, and potential clients can open doors to new opportunities, partnerships, and collaborations.

Attending industry events, joining professional organizations, and participating in online communities can help entrepreneurs expand their networks and stay connected with the latest trends and developments in their fields. Collaborating with others can also lead to the sharing of resources, knowledge, and expertise, which can be invaluable in navigating the challenges of entrepreneurship.

5.3.6 Government Support and Resources

Governments play a crucial role in supporting entrepreneurship and self-employment in a jobless era. They can provide resources, funding, and mentorship programs to help aspiring entrepreneurs start and grow their businesses. Additionally, governments can create policies and regulations that foster a favorable environment for entrepreneurship, such as reducing bureaucratic hurdles and providing tax incentives.

Entrepreneurs should take advantage of these government initiatives and seek out the available support. By leveraging these resources, entrepreneurs can access valuable guidance, funding opportunities, and networking platforms that can significantly enhance their chances of success.

5.3.7 The Future of Entrepreneurship

As the job market continues to evolve, entrepreneurship and self-employment will play an increasingly vital role in the future of work. The ability to adapt, innovate, and create value will be highly sought after skills. By embracing entrepreneurship, individuals can take control of their own destinies, create meaningful work, and contribute to the economic growth and development of society.

In conclusion, entrepreneurship and self-employment offer individuals a pathway to navigate the jobless era.

● ● ●

By embracing innovation, developing diverse skill sets, building strong networks, and leveraging government support, aspiring entrepreneurs can overcome challenges and create successful businesses. The future belongs to those who are willing to take risks, think creatively, and seize the opportunities that arise in a changing job market.

5.4 Building Resilience in a Changing Job Market

In a rapidly changing job market, building resilience is crucial for individuals to navigate the uncertainties and challenges that come with technological advancements and automation. As the nature of work continues to evolve, it is essential to develop the skills and mindset necessary to adapt and thrive in this new era. This section will explore strategies and approaches to building resilience in the face of a changing job market.

5.4.1 Embracing Lifelong Learning

One of the key ways to build resilience in a changing job market is through embracing lifelong learning. As technology continues to advance and industries transform, the demand for new skills and knowledge is constantly evolving. By adopting a mindset of continuous learning, individuals can stay ahead of the curve and remain relevant in the job market.

Lifelong learning involves actively seeking out opportunities to acquire new skills, whether through formal education, online courses, workshops, or self-study. It is important to identify the skills that are in demand and align them with personal interests and strengths. By investing time and effort into learning new skills, individuals can enhance their employability and adaptability to changing job requirements.

5.4.2 Developing Transferable Skills

In a job market where specific roles may become obsolete, developing transferable skills is essential for building resilience. Transferable skills are those that can be applied across different industries and job roles. These skills include critical thinking, problem-solving, communication, collaboration, adaptability, and leadership.

By focusing on developing transferable skills, individuals can position themselves as valuable assets to employers, regardless of the specific job or industry. These skills enable individuals to adapt to new roles and responsibilities, making them more resilient in the face of job market changes. Additionally, transferable skills are often highly sought after by employers as they contribute to a more agile and versatile workforce.

5.4.3 Cultivating a Growth Mindset

Building resilience in a changing job market also requires cultivating a growth mindset. A growth mindset is the belief that abilities and intelligence can be developed through dedication and hard work. It is the understanding that failures and setbacks are opportunities for learning and growth.

By adopting a growth mindset, individuals can embrace challenges and view them as opportunities to develop new skills and knowledge. This mindset encourages individuals to persist in the face of obstacles, seek feedback, and continuously improve. Cultivating a growth mindset allows individuals to adapt to changing circumstances and bounce back from setbacks, making them more resilient in the job market.

5.4.4 Building a Professional Network

In a changing job market, building a strong professional network is crucial for resilience. Networking provides opportunities for career development, job referrals, and access to information about emerging job trends and opportunities. By connecting with professionals in various industries, individuals can stay informed about changes in the job market and gain insights into potential career paths.

Building a professional network can be done through attending industry events, joining professional associations, participating in online communities, and leveraging social media platforms like LinkedIn. It is important to actively engage with network connections, share knowledge, and offer support to others. A robust professional network can provide a support system during times of transition and help individuals navigate the changing job market with greater resilience.

5.4.5 Embracing Entrepreneurship and Side Hustles

In a changing job market, embracing entrepreneurship and side hustles can provide individuals with additional sources of income and increased resilience. Starting a business or pursuing a side hustle allows individuals to diversify their income streams and gain valuable entrepreneurial skills.

Entrepreneurship and side hustles also offer the flexibility to adapt to changing market demands and pursue opportunities that align with personal interests and passions. They provide individuals with a sense of control over their career trajectory and can serve as a safety net during periods of job market instability.

5.4.6 Prioritizing Well-being and Self-care

Building resilience in a changing job market goes beyond professional development; it also involves prioritizing well-being and self-care. The stress and uncertainty that come with job market changes can take a toll on individuals' mental and physical health. Therefore, it is essential to prioritize self-care practices that promote overall well-being.

This can include activities such as exercise, meditation, spending time with loved ones, pursuing hobbies, and maintaining a healthy work-life balance. Taking care of one's physical and mental health allows individuals to better cope with the challenges of a changing job market and maintain a positive outlook.

5.4.7 Seeking Support and Mentorship

Lastly, building resilience in a changing job market involves seeking support and mentorship. Connecting with mentors who have experience navigating similar challenges can provide valuable guidance and insights.

Mentors can offer advice, share their own experiences, and provide support during times of uncertainty.

Additionally, seeking support from friends, family, and professional networks can help individuals navigate the emotional and practical aspects of a changing job market. Sharing concerns, seeking feedback, and collaborating with others can provide a sense of community and support, enhancing resilience in the face of job market changes.

By embracing lifelong learning, developing transferable skills, cultivating a growth mindset, building a professional network, embracing entrepreneurship, prioritizing well-being, and seeking support, individuals can build resilience in a changing job market. These strategies empower individuals to adapt, thrive, and find new opportunities in the evolving world of work.

6

Ethical Considerations

6.1 Ethics in Automation and Artificial Intelligence

As automation and artificial intelligence (AI) continue to advance, the ethical implications surrounding their use become increasingly important. The integration of these technologies into various industries has the potential to revolutionize the way we work and live. However, it also raises concerns about the impact on employment, privacy, and the overall well-being of society. In this section, we will explore the ethical considerations surrounding automation and AI, and discuss the need for responsible implementation and regulation.

6.1.1 The Ethical Dilemma

The rise of automation and AI presents a significant ethical dilemma. On one hand, these technologies have the potential to improve efficiency, productivity, and overall quality of life. They can perform tasks more accurately and at a faster pace than humans, leading to increased output and economic growth. However, the widespread adoption of automation and AI also threatens to displace human workers, leading to unemployment and income inequality.

6.1.2 Job Displacement and Unemployment

One of the primary ethical concerns surrounding automation and AI is the potential for job displacement and unemployment. As machines and algorithms become more capable, they can replace human workers in various industries, leading to a significant reduction in available jobs. This raises questions about the responsibility of companies and governments to ensure that the benefits of automation are shared equitably and that those who are displaced are provided with alternative opportunities for employment or support.

6.1.3 Algorithmic Bias and Discrimination

Another ethical consideration in automation and AI is the issue of algorithmic bias and discrimination. Algorithms are designed to make decisions based on patterns and data, but they can inadvertently perpetuate biases present in the data they are trained on. This can lead to discriminatory outcomes in areas such as hiring, lending, and criminal justice. It is crucial to address these biases and ensure that algorithms are fair, transparent, and accountable.

6.1.4 Privacy and Data Security

The increasing reliance on automation and AI also raises concerns about privacy and data security. These technologies often require access to vast amounts of personal data to function effectively. However, the collection, storage, and use of this data can pose risks to individuals' privacy and security. It is essential to establish robust regulations and safeguards to protect personal information and prevent its misuse.

6.1.5 Ethical Decision-Making in AI

To address the ethical challenges posed by automation and AI, it is crucial to incorporate ethical decision-making frameworks into the development and deployment of these technologies. Ethical considerations should be integrated into the design process, ensuring that AI systems are developed with a focus on fairness, transparency, and accountability. This includes involving diverse perspectives and stakeholders in the decision-making process to mitigate biases and ensure that the technology serves the best interests of society as a whole.

6.1.6 Responsible AI Governance

Responsible AI governance is essential to ensure that automation and AI are used ethically and for the benefit of society. This involves establishing regulations and standards that govern the development, deployment, and use of these technologies. Governments, industry leaders, and experts must collaborate to create frameworks that address the ethical concerns surrounding automation and AI, while also fostering innovation and economic growth.

6.1.7 Ethical Considerations in Autonomous Systems

As automation and AI advance, the development of autonomous systems becomes a reality. These systems, such as self-driving cars and autonomous drones, raise unique ethical considerations. Questions arise regarding the responsibility and accountability of these systems in making decisions that may impact human lives. It is crucial to establish guidelines and regulations that ensure the safe and ethical operation of autonomous systems, prioritizing human safety and well-being.

6.1.8 The Role of Education and Awareness

Education and awareness play a vital role in addressing the ethical challenges of automation and AI. It is essential to educate individuals about the potential benefits and risks associated with these technologies. This includes promoting digital literacy, teaching critical thinking skills, and fostering a broader understanding of the ethical implications of automation and AI. By empowering individuals with knowledge, we can create a more informed and responsible society that actively participates in shaping the future of automation and AI.

In conclusion, the ethical considerations surrounding automation and artificial intelligence are of paramount importance in the jobless era. As these technologies continue to shape our world, it is crucial to ensure that their implementation is guided by principles of fairness, transparency, and accountability. By addressing the ethical dilemmas associated with automation and AI, we can create a future that benefits all of humanity, while also embracing the potential for innovation and progress.

6.2 Ensuring Fairness and Equity

As we navigate the jobless era, it is crucial to prioritize fairness and equity in our approach to the changing world of work. The rise of automation and the subsequent displacement of jobs have the potential to exacerbate existing inequalities and create new ones. To ensure a just and inclusive society, we must address these challenges head-on and implement measures that promote fairness and equity for all.

6.2.1 Reducing Bias in Hiring and Recruitment

One of the key areas where fairness and equity must be prioritized is in the hiring and recruitment process. As technology plays an increasingly significant role in these processes, it is essential to ensure that algorithms and AI systems used for candidate selection are free from bias. Bias in hiring can perpetuate existing inequalities and limit opportunities for underrepresented groups.

To address this issue, organizations should invest in developing and implementing algorithms that are designed to be fair and unbiased. This requires careful consideration of the data used to train these systems and ongoing monitoring to identify and rectify any biases that may emerge. Additionally, organizations should strive to create diverse hiring teams that can provide different perspectives and challenge potential biases in the decision-making process.

6.2.2 Promoting Equal Access to Education and Training

In a jobless era, access to education and training becomes even more critical. To ensure fairness and equity, it is essential to provide equal opportunities for individuals to acquire the skills and knowledge needed to thrive in the changing job market. This includes addressing barriers such as affordability, geographical location, and social disparities.

Governments and educational institutions should work together to develop comprehensive and accessible education and training programs. This may involve initiatives such as providing financial assistance for those who cannot afford traditional education, expanding online learning platforms, and establishing community-based training centers in underserved areas. By promoting equal access to education and training, we can empower individuals from all backgrounds to adapt and succeed in the jobless era.

6.2.3 Fostering Inclusive Entrepreneurship

Entrepreneurship can be a pathway to economic independence and empowerment. However, it is crucial to ensure that opportunities for entrepreneurship are accessible to all, regardless of background or socioeconomic status. In a jobless era, fostering inclusive entrepreneurship becomes even more important as traditional employment opportunities decline.

● ● ●

To promote fairness and equity in entrepreneurship, governments and organizations should provide support and resources to underrepresented groups. This may include mentorship programs, access to capital and funding, and targeted training initiatives. By creating an inclusive entrepreneurial ecosystem, we can empower individuals from diverse backgrounds to create their own opportunities and contribute to the economy.

6.2.4 Addressing Income Inequality

The jobless era has the potential to widen income inequality if left unchecked. As automation replaces jobs, it is crucial to implement measures that ensure a fair distribution of wealth and resources. This may involve policies such as progressive taxation, wealth redistribution, and the implementation of a universal basic income.

By addressing income inequality, we can mitigate the negative social and economic consequences of joblessness. It is essential to create a society where everyone has access to basic necessities and opportunities for upward mobility. This requires a collective effort from governments, businesses, and individuals to prioritize fairness and equity in economic policies and practices.

6.2.5 Empowering Workers in the Gig Economy

The gig economy has emerged as a significant component of the jobless era. While it offers flexibility and opportunities for some, it also presents challenges in terms of job security, benefits, and fair compensation.

To ensure fairness and equity in the gig economy, it is crucial to empower workers and provide them with adequate protections.

This can be achieved through the implementation of regulations that guarantee fair wages, benefits, and working conditions for gig workers. Additionally, platforms and companies operating in the gig economy should be held accountable for ensuring the well-being and rights of their workers. By empowering gig workers, we can create a more equitable and just work environment for all.

In conclusion, ensuring fairness and equity in the jobless era is essential for creating a just and inclusive society. By reducing bias in hiring, promoting equal access to education and training, fostering inclusive entrepreneurship, addressing income inequality, and empowering workers in the gig economy, we can navigate the challenges of automation and joblessness while prioritizing the well-being and opportunities of all individuals. It is through these efforts that we can build a future where fairness and equity are at the core of our evolving world of work.

6.3 Addressing Bias and Discrimination

As we navigate the jobless era, it is crucial to address the issue of bias and discrimination that may arise in the changing landscape of work. While automation and technology have the potential to revolutionize industries and improve efficiency, they also have the potential to perpetuate and amplify existing biases and discrimination.

● ● ●

6.3.1 The Impact of Bias in Automation

Automation systems are designed and programmed by humans, and as such, they can inherit the biases and prejudices of their creators. If not carefully monitored and regulated, these biases can be embedded into algorithms and decision-making processes, leading to discriminatory outcomes. For example, if a hiring algorithm is trained on biased historical data, it may perpetuate existing inequalities by favoring certain demographics or excluding others.

6.3.2 Recognizing and Mitigating Bias

To address bias and discrimination in the jobless era, it is essential to recognize and understand the potential sources of bias. This includes acknowledging the biases that may exist within the data used to train algorithms, as well as the biases that may be present in the design and implementation of automated systems.

One approach to mitigating bias is to ensure diverse representation in the development and decision-making processes. By involving individuals from different backgrounds and perspectives, it is possible to identify and challenge biases before they become embedded in automated systems. Additionally, ongoing monitoring and evaluation of automated systems can help identify and rectify any discriminatory outcomes.

6.3.3 Ethical Guidelines and Standards

In order to address bias and discrimination in the jobless era, it is crucial to establish ethical guidelines and standards for the development and deployment of automated systems. These guidelines should prioritize fairness, transparency, and accountability.

Ethical guidelines can include requirements for transparency in algorithmic decision-making, ensuring that individuals understand how decisions are being made and have the ability to challenge them. They can also include provisions for regular audits and evaluations of automated systems to identify and rectify any biases or discriminatory outcomes.

6.3.4 Regulation and Oversight

Government regulation and oversight play a vital role in addressing bias and discrimination in the jobless era. It is essential for policymakers to stay informed about the latest advancements in automation and technology and to develop regulations that protect individuals from discriminatory practices.

Regulations can include requirements for companies to conduct regular audits of their automated systems to identify and address biases. They can also mandate the collection and reporting of data on the impact of automation on different demographic groups to ensure that disparities are identified and addressed.

6.3.5 Education and Awareness

Education and awareness are key components in addressing bias and discrimination in the jobless era. It is important to educate individuals about the potential biases and discriminatory practices that may arise in automated systems. This includes providing training on how to recognize and challenge bias, as well as promoting awareness of the importance of diversity and inclusion in the development and deployment of automated systems.

By fostering a culture of awareness and understanding, individuals can become active participants in addressing bias and discrimination. This can include advocating for ethical practices within their organizations, supporting policies and regulations that promote fairness and equity, and actively challenging biased decision-making processes.

6.3.6 Collaboration and Partnerships

Addressing bias and discrimination in the jobless era requires collaboration and partnerships between various stakeholders. This includes collaboration between technology companies, policymakers, researchers, and advocacy groups.

By working together, these stakeholders can share knowledge and best practices, develop standards and guidelines, and advocate for policies that prioritize fairness and equity. Collaboration can also help ensure that the voices and perspectives of marginalized communities are included in the development and deployment of automated systems.

6.3.7 The Role of Individuals

Individuals also have a role to play in addressing bias and discrimination in the jobless era. By being aware of their own biases and actively challenging them, individuals can contribute to creating a more inclusive and equitable future.

This includes being mindful of the potential biases in their decision-making processes, seeking out diverse perspectives, and advocating for fairness and equity within their organizations. Individuals can also support initiatives and organizations that are working towards addressing bias and discrimination in the jobless era.

In conclusion, addressing bias and discrimination in the jobless era is crucial to ensure a fair and equitable future of work. By recognizing and mitigating bias, establishing ethical guidelines and standards, implementing regulation and oversight, promoting education and awareness, fostering collaboration and partnerships, and taking individual responsibility, we can work towards creating a future where automation and technology are used to enhance human potential rather than perpetuate inequality.

6.4 The Role of Ethics in a Jobless Society

As we navigate the uncharted waters of a jobless society, it becomes increasingly important to consider the ethical implications of this new era. The rapid advancement of automation and artificial intelligence has led to a significant reduction in traditional employment opportunities, leaving many individuals without a means to support themselves and their families. In this chapter, we will explore the role of ethics in a jobless society and discuss the ethical considerations that arise in this new landscape.

● ● ●

6.4.1 Ethical Dilemmas in a Jobless Society

The rise of automation and the subsequent loss of jobs present a range of ethical dilemmas that society must grapple with. One of the primary concerns is the potential for increased income inequality and wealth disparity. As automation replaces human labor, those who own and control the technology stand to benefit greatly, while those who are displaced face economic hardship. This raises questions about fairness and equity in a society where a small percentage of individuals hold the majority of wealth and power.

Another ethical dilemma is the impact of joblessness on individuals' sense of self-worth and dignity. Work has long been a source of identity and purpose for many people, and the loss of employment can lead to feelings of worthlessness and despair. It is crucial to address these psychological and emotional consequences and find ways to support individuals in maintaining their sense of self-worth and dignity.

6.4.2 Ethical Responsibilities of Governments and Corporations

In a jobless society, the role of governments and corporations becomes even more critical in ensuring the well-being of their citizens and employees. Governments have an ethical responsibility to create policies and programs that address the challenges of unemployment and income inequality. This may include implementing social safety nets, providing retraining and education opportunities, and exploring alternative economic models such as universal basic income.

Corporations, on the other hand, have a responsibility to prioritize the welfare of their employees and the communities they operate in. This includes ethical considerations such as fair compensation, providing opportunities for upskilling and reskilling, and actively contributing to the social and economic development of the regions they operate in. By embracing ethical practices, corporations can help mitigate the negative impacts of joblessness and contribute to a more equitable society.

6.4.3 Ethical Use of Automation and Artificial Intelligence

As automation and artificial intelligence continue to advance, it is crucial to consider the ethical implications of their use. Ethical guidelines should be established to ensure that these technologies are developed and deployed in a manner that benefits society as a whole. This includes addressing issues such as privacy, data security, and the potential for bias and discrimination in algorithmic decision-making.

Additionally, ethical considerations should be given to the impact of automation on the environment. While automation can lead to increased efficiency and productivity, it can also contribute to resource depletion and environmental degradation. It is essential to develop and implement sustainable practices that minimize the negative environmental impacts of automation.

6.4.4 Promoting Human Values and Well-being

In a jobless society, it becomes even more crucial to prioritize human values and well-being. As technology takes over routine and repetitive tasks, there is an opportunity to focus on developing and utilizing uniquely human skills such as creativity, critical thinking, and emotional intelligence. By emphasizing these skills, we can create a society that values human connection, empathy, and personal growth.

Education and training play a vital role in promoting these human values. It is essential to reimagine education systems to equip individuals with the skills necessary to thrive in a jobless society. This includes fostering creativity, encouraging lifelong learning, and promoting adaptability and resilience. By prioritizing these values, we can create a society that values the holistic well-being of its citizens.

6.4.5 Ethical Considerations in Redefining Work

In a jobless society, the concept of work itself undergoes a transformation. It is crucial to consider the ethical implications of this redefinition. Work has long been associated with productivity and contribution to society, and it is essential to ensure that individuals continue to find meaning and purpose in their lives.

One ethical consideration is the need to redefine societal attitudes towards work. Rather than valuing individuals solely based on their employment status, we should recognize and appreciate the diverse contributions individuals make to society, whether

● ● ●

through paid work, caregiving, volunteering, or other forms of meaningful engagement.

Another ethical consideration is the importance of providing individuals with opportunities for personal growth and self-actualization. In a jobless society, individuals may have more time and freedom to pursue their passions and interests. It is crucial to create a society that supports and encourages individuals in their pursuit of personal fulfillment and self-expression.

6.4.6 Ethical Decision-Making in a Jobless Society

In a jobless society, ethical decision-making becomes even more critical. Individuals, organizations, and governments must consider the broader societal implications of their actions. This includes considering the impact on individuals who are displaced by automation, the potential for increased inequality, and the long-term sustainability of our economic and social systems.

Ethical decision-making also requires a commitment to transparency and accountability. It is essential for organizations and governments to be open and honest about their intentions and actions, and to actively seek input and feedback from those affected by their decisions. By fostering a culture of transparency and accountability, we can ensure that ethical considerations are at the forefront of decision-making processes.

In conclusion, the role of ethics in a jobless society is paramount. As we navigate the challenges and

● ● ●
110

opportunities presented by automation and artificial intelligence, it is crucial to prioritize fairness, equity, and the well-being of individuals and society as a whole. By embracing ethical practices and considering the broader societal implications of our actions, we can create a future that is both technologically advanced and ethically sound.

7

The Future of Work-Life Balance

7.1 Redefining Work-Life Balance

In the jobless era, where automation and technological advancements have rendered many traditional jobs obsolete, the concept of work-life balance takes on a whole new meaning. With fewer people engaged in traditional employment, the boundaries between work and personal life become blurred, and individuals are faced with the challenge of redefining what work means to them and how it fits into their overall lifestyle.

The Evolving Definition of Work

In a jobless society, work is no longer solely defined by traditional employment. Instead, it encompasses a broader range of activities that contribute to personal growth, fulfillment, and the betterment of society as a whole. People are encouraged to explore their passions, pursue creative endeavors, and engage in meaningful projects that align with their values and interests.

Embracing Flexibility and Autonomy

With the decline of traditional employment, individuals have the opportunity to embrace flexible work arrangements that suit their unique needs and preferences. The rigid 9-to-5 schedule becomes a thing of the past, as people have the freedom to choose when, where, and how they work. This newfound autonomy allows individuals to prioritize their personal lives, spend more time with loved ones, and pursue personal interests while still engaging in meaningful work.

Balancing Multiple Roles and Responsibilities

In a jobless era, individuals are no longer defined solely by their professional roles. They have the freedom to explore and embrace multiple roles and responsibilities, such as being caregivers, volunteers, entrepreneurs, or community leaders. This shift in focus from a single career to a multifaceted life allows individuals to find fulfillment in various aspects of their lives and create a more balanced and holistic approach to work and personal commitments.

Reducing Stress and Burnout

The traditional work model often leads to high levels of stress and burnout due to long hours, demanding deadlines, and the pressure to constantly perform. In a jobless society, individuals have the opportunity to prioritize their well-being and mental health. With the ability to set their own schedules and choose work that aligns with their passions, individuals can reduce stress levels and create a healthier work-life balance.

● ● ●

Emphasizing Leisure and Recreation

In a world where work is no longer the primary focus, leisure and recreation take on a more significant role in people's lives. Individuals have more time to engage in activities they enjoy, such as pursuing hobbies, traveling, spending time in nature, or simply relaxing and rejuvenating. The emphasis on leisure and recreation not only enhances personal well-being but also fosters creativity, inspiration, and a sense of fulfillment.

Finding Meaning and Purpose

With the traditional notion of work being challenged, individuals are encouraged to seek meaning and purpose in their lives beyond their professional endeavors. They have the opportunity to explore their passions, contribute to causes they believe in, and make a positive impact on their communities. This shift in focus from simply earning a living to finding personal fulfillment and making a difference in the world allows individuals to lead more purpose-driven lives.

Nurturing Relationships and Connection

In a jobless era, where the focus is on personal growth and fulfillment, relationships and human connection become even more vital. With more time available, individuals can invest in building and nurturing meaningful relationships with family, friends, and their communities. Strong social connections not only provide support and happiness but also contribute to overall well-being and a sense of belonging.

●●●

Embracing a Holistic Approach

Redefining work-life balance in a jobless society requires embracing a holistic approach that considers all aspects of an individual's life. It involves integrating work, personal life, leisure, relationships, and personal growth into a cohesive and fulfilling whole. This holistic approach allows individuals to lead more balanced, meaningful, and satisfying lives.

As we navigate the jobless era, it is essential to recognize that work-life balance is no longer solely about separating work from personal life. It is about finding harmony, fulfillment, and purpose in all aspects of our lives. By embracing flexibility, nurturing relationships, prioritizing well-being, and pursuing meaningful endeavors, we can redefine work-life balance and create a future that is not only jobless but also fulfilling and enriching.

7.2 Flexible Work Arrangements

In the jobless era, where automation and technological advancements have significantly impacted the job market, traditional work arrangements are being redefined. The concept of a 9-to-5 job in a fixed location is gradually giving way to more flexible work arrangements. These arrangements offer individuals the freedom to choose when, where, and how they work, providing a better work-life balance and increased autonomy.

7.2.1 The Rise of Remote Work

One of the most prominent flexible work arrangements is remote work. With the advent of high-speed internet and advanced communication tools, working from home or any location outside of a traditional office has become increasingly feasible. Remote work offers numerous benefits to both employees and employers.

For employees, remote work eliminates the need for commuting, saving valuable time and reducing stress. It allows individuals to create a personalized work environment that suits their preferences and needs. Remote work also enables a better work-life balance, as it provides the flexibility to manage personal and professional responsibilities more effectively.

Employers also benefit from remote work arrangements. They can tap into a global talent pool, accessing skilled professionals from different geographical locations. Remote work often leads to increased productivity, as employees have fewer distractions and can focus on their tasks without interruptions. Additionally, companies can save on office space and related expenses, contributing to cost reduction.

7.2.2 Flextime and Compressed Workweeks

Flextime is another flexible work arrangement that allows employees to choose their working hours within certain limits. Instead of adhering to a fixed schedule, individuals can start and finish their workday at different times. This arrangement recognizes that people have different peak productivity periods and personal commitments outside of work.

By offering flextime, employers can accommodate the diverse needs of their workforce. It promotes a healthier work-life balance by allowing employees to attend to personal matters, such as family obligations or pursuing hobbies, without sacrificing their professional responsibilities. Flextime also enhances employee satisfaction and morale, leading to increased loyalty and productivity.

Compressed workweeks are another form of flexible work arrangement that condenses the standard workweek into fewer days. For example, instead of working five eight-hour days, employees may work four ten-hour days. This arrangement provides individuals with longer weekends, allowing for more leisure time and the opportunity to pursue personal interests.

Compressed workweeks can be particularly beneficial for employees who have long commutes or desire more uninterrupted time for personal activities. It can also contribute to reducing energy consumption and traffic congestion, as fewer commuting days result in decreased transportation needs.

7.2.3 Job Sharing and Part-Time Work

Job sharing is a flexible work arrangement where two or more employees share the responsibilities of a single full-time position. Each employee works part-time, dividing the workload and collaborating to ensure a seamless transition between shifts. Job sharing allows individuals to maintain a work-life balance while still contributing to the workforce.

This arrangement benefits both employees and employers. Employees can pursue personal interests or fulfill caregiving responsibilities while remaining engaged in the workforce. Employers, on the other hand, can retain experienced employees who may have otherwise left due to personal circumstances. Job sharing also promotes knowledge sharing and collaboration, as employees work closely together to ensure continuity in their shared role.

Part-time work is another flexible arrangement that allows individuals to work fewer hours than a standard full-time position. It provides individuals with the opportunity to balance work with personal commitments or pursue additional education or training. Part-time work is particularly attractive to parents with young children, students, or individuals transitioning into retirement.

Employers can benefit from part-time work arrangements by accessing a wider pool of talent and reducing labor costs. Part-time employees often bring unique perspectives and diverse skill sets to the workforce, contributing to increased creativity and innovation within the organization.

7.2.4 Freelancing and the Gig Economy

Freelancing and the gig economy have experienced significant growth in recent years. These flexible work arrangements involve individuals working on a project or task basis, often for multiple clients or companies. Freelancers have the freedom to choose the projects they work on, set their rates, and determine their own schedules.

The gig economy provides individuals with the opportunity to pursue their passions and leverage their skills in a flexible manner. It allows for greater control over one's work-life balance and the potential to earn a higher income based on performance and demand. Freelancers also have the advantage of working with a variety of clients, gaining diverse experiences and expanding their professional network.

For businesses, freelancers offer a cost-effective solution to meet specific project needs without the long-term commitment of hiring full-time employees. They can tap into specialized skills and expertise on-demand, ensuring efficient project completion. The gig economy also fosters innovation and entrepreneurship, as individuals have the freedom to explore new ideas and create their own opportunities.

Conclusion

Flexible work arrangements are becoming increasingly prevalent in the jobless era. Remote work, flextime, compressed workweeks, job sharing, part-time work, freelancing, and the gig economy offer individuals the freedom to design their work lives according to their preferences and needs. These arrangements promote a better work-life balance, increased autonomy, and the opportunity to pursue personal interests and passions. As the job market continues to evolve, embracing flexible work arrangements will be crucial in creating a positive future where individuals can thrive both personally and professionally.

7.3 The Importance of Leisure and Recreation

In a jobless era, where automation and technology have taken over many traditional jobs, the concept of leisure and recreation becomes even more crucial. As the nature of work changes and the traditional 9-to-5 job becomes less prevalent, individuals have more time and freedom to explore their personal interests, hobbies, and passions. This shift in the job market presents an opportunity for people to redefine their work-life balance and find fulfillment outside of traditional employment.

The Benefits of Leisure and Recreation

Leisure and recreation activities play a vital role in maintaining physical, mental, and emotional well-being. Engaging in activities that bring joy, relaxation, and personal growth can have numerous benefits, especially in a jobless society. Here are some of the key advantages:

1. Stress Reduction and Mental Health

Leisure and recreation provide an escape from the pressures and stresses of daily life. Engaging in activities such as sports, hobbies, or creative pursuits can help reduce anxiety, improve mood, and enhance overall mental well-being. Taking time for leisure allows individuals to recharge and rejuvenate, leading to increased productivity and a better ability to cope with challenges.

2. Personal Growth and Skill Development

With more time on their hands, individuals can dedicate themselves to personal growth and skill development. Pursuing hobbies and interests can lead to the acquisition of new skills and knowledge, fostering a sense of accomplishment and self-improvement. Whether it's learning a musical instrument, painting, writing, or exploring new sports, leisure activities provide opportunities for continuous learning and personal development.

3. Enhanced Relationships and Social Connections

Leisure and recreation activities often involve social interaction, which is essential for building and maintaining relationships. In a jobless era, where traditional workplace connections may be limited, engaging in leisure activities can help individuals forge new friendships and strengthen existing bonds. Participating in group activities, clubs, or community events provides opportunities for socializing, networking, and creating a sense of belonging.

4. Improved Physical Health

Many leisure and recreation activities involve physical movement and exercise, contributing to improved physical health. Engaging in regular physical activity not only helps maintain a healthy weight but also reduces the risk of chronic diseases, boosts

● ● ●

cardiovascular health, and enhances overall fitness levels. Whether it's hiking, swimming, dancing, or practicing yoga, incorporating physical activities into leisure time can have significant long-term health benefits.

5. Increased Creativity and Innovation

Leisure and recreation provide a fertile ground for creativity and innovation. When individuals have the freedom to explore their interests and passions, they often discover new ideas, perspectives, and solutions. Engaging in creative activities such as writing, painting, or experimenting with new technologies can stimulate the imagination and foster innovative thinking. This creativity can spill over into other areas of life, including work and problem-solving.

Balancing Leisure and Work

While leisure and recreation are essential for personal well-being, it is crucial to strike a balance between leisure and work in a jobless era. Here are some strategies to ensure a healthy equilibrium:

1. Time Management

Effective time management is key to balancing leisure and work. By setting clear boundaries and allocating specific time for leisure activities, individuals can ensure they have dedicated periods for relaxation and personal pursuits. Planning and prioritizing tasks can help prevent leisure time from being overshadowed by work-related responsibilities.

2. Prioritizing Self-Care

In a society where work is no longer the primary source of identity and purpose, individuals must prioritize self-care. This includes taking care of physical health, mental well-being, and emotional needs. Engaging in leisure activities that promote self-care, such as meditation, mindfulness, or spa treatments, can help individuals recharge and maintain a healthy work-life balance.

3. Exploring New Interests and Hobbies

With more time available, individuals can explore new interests and hobbies that bring them joy and fulfillment. Trying out different activities and discovering new passions can add excitement and variety to life. Whether it's learning a new language, taking up photography, or joining a sports team, embracing new experiences can enrich leisure time and provide a sense of purpose.

4. Disconnecting from Technology

While technology has its benefits, it can also be a source of distraction and overstimulation. To fully enjoy leisure and recreation, it is essential to disconnect from technology periodically. Setting aside designated tech-free time allows individuals to be fully present in their leisure activities, fostering a deeper sense of relaxation and enjoyment.

5. Embracing a Healthy Work-Life Integration

In a jobless era, the boundaries between work and leisure can become blurred. Embracing a healthy work-life integration involves finding ways to incorporate leisure activities into daily life, even if they are related to work or personal projects. This approach allows individuals to find meaning and purpose in their leisure time while still pursuing their passions and interests.

Conclusion

In a jobless era, the importance of leisure and recreation cannot be overstated. As traditional jobs become scarce, individuals have the opportunity to redefine their work-life balance and explore new avenues of personal fulfillment. Engaging in leisure activities not only promotes physical and mental well-being but also fosters personal growth, creativity, and social connections. By striking a balance between leisure and work, individuals can lead fulfilling lives and embrace the possibilities of a jobless future.

7.4 Finding Meaning and Purpose in a Jobless Era

In a jobless era where automation and technology have taken over many traditional jobs, finding meaning and purpose in our lives becomes even more crucial. With the rise of unemployment and the changing nature of work, it is essential to explore new avenues for personal fulfillment and satisfaction. This chapter delves into the importance of finding meaning and purpose in a jobless era and provides insights into how individuals can navigate this new landscape.

7.4.1 Redefining Success

In a society that has long equated success with traditional employment and financial stability, redefining success becomes imperative in a jobless era. Instead of measuring success solely based on job titles or income, individuals can shift their focus towards personal growth, self-fulfillment, and contributing to the well-being of society. This redefinition allows individuals to explore alternative paths and pursue their passions, ultimately leading to a more fulfilling and purposeful life.

7.4.2 Pursuing Personal Passions

With the freedom from traditional employment, individuals have the opportunity to pursue their personal passions and interests. Whether it is art, music, writing, or any other creative endeavor, the jobless era provides the time and flexibility to explore these passions on a deeper level. Engaging in activities that bring joy and fulfillment not only enhances personal well-being but also contributes to the overall cultural and artistic landscape of society.

7.4.3 Volunteering and Community Engagement

In a jobless era, individuals can find meaning and purpose by actively engaging in their communities through volunteering and social initiatives. By dedicating their time and skills to causes they believe in, individuals can make a positive impact on society and create a sense of purpose. Volunteering not only benefits the community but also provides individuals with a sense of fulfillment and connection with others who share similar values and goals.

7.4.4 Lifelong Learning and Personal Development

In a rapidly changing world, continuous learning and personal development are essential for finding meaning and purpose. With the availability of online courses, workshops, and resources, individuals can acquire new skills, expand their knowledge, and stay relevant in a jobless era. Engaging in lifelong learning not only enhances personal growth but also opens up new opportunities for personal and professional development.

7.4.5 Entrepreneurship and Innovation

The jobless era presents a unique opportunity for individuals to explore entrepreneurship and innovation. With the freedom to pursue their own ventures, individuals can create businesses that align with their values and passions. Entrepreneurship allows individuals to take control of their own destiny, create meaningful work, and contribute to the economy in innovative ways. By embracing entrepreneurship, individuals can find purpose and fulfillment in building something of their own.

7.4.6 Embracing a Balanced Lifestyle

In a jobless era, it is crucial to prioritize a balanced lifestyle that encompasses not only work but also leisure, relationships, and personal well-being. Finding meaning and purpose requires individuals to take care of their physical, mental, and emotional health. This can be achieved through activities such as exercise, mindfulness practices, spending quality time with loved ones, and pursuing hobbies and interests outside of work. By embracing a balanced lifestyle, individuals can find fulfillment in all aspects of their lives.

7.4.7 Contributing to the Greater Good

Finding meaning and purpose in a jobless era also involves contributing to the greater good of society. Individuals can engage in social and environmental initiatives that align with their values and make a positive impact on the world. Whether it is advocating for social justice, promoting sustainability, or supporting charitable causes, contributing to the greater good provides a sense of purpose and fulfillment that goes beyond traditional employment.

7.4.8 Cultivating Meaningful Relationships

In a jobless era, cultivating meaningful relationships becomes even more important. With the changing nature of work and the potential for isolation, individuals need to prioritize building and nurturing relationships with others. Meaningful connections with family, friends, and communities provide support, companionship, and a sense of belonging. These relationships contribute to personal well-being and provide a sense of purpose and fulfillment in a jobless era.

7.4.9 Embracing Personal Growth and Adaptability

In a rapidly evolving world, embracing personal growth and adaptability is crucial for finding meaning and purpose. Individuals need to be open to new experiences, willing to learn from failures, and adaptable to changing circumstances. By continuously evolving and growing, individuals can navigate the challenges of a jobless era with resilience and find meaning in the process of personal development.

7.4.10 Reflecting on Values and Priorities

In a jobless era, it is essential for individuals to reflect on their values and priorities. By understanding what truly matters to them, individuals can make intentional choices that align with their core beliefs and aspirations. This self-reflection allows individuals to make decisions that lead to a more meaningful and purposeful life, even in the absence of traditional employment.

As we navigate the jobless era, it is crucial to remember that finding meaning and purpose goes beyond traditional notions of work. By redefining success, pursuing personal passions, engaging in community initiatives, embracing personal growth, and cultivating meaningful relationships, individuals can thrive in a jobless era and create a fulfilling and purposeful life.

8

Employment crises in history and how they have been addressed

8.1 employment crises in history

Throughout history, there have been various periods characterized by significant unemployment in the workforce. These periods often coincide with economic downturns, technological shifts, or major geopolitical events. Here are some notable historical periods of high unemployment and their associated reasons:

8.1.1 Great Depression (1929-1930s):

The most famous and severe economic downturn in modern history, the Great Depression, resulted in widespread unemployment. The stock market crash of 1929, combined with bank failures and a lack of effective economic policies, led to a sharp contraction in economic activity. Unemployment rates in some countries soared to over 25%.

8.1.2 Post-World War I (1919-1920):

Following World War I, many countries experienced a brief but severe recession. The demobilization of soldiers and the shift from wartime to peacetime production contributed to economic challenges and high unemployment.

8.1.3 Oil Crisis (1970s):

The oil shocks of the 1970s, caused by geopolitical events in the Middle East, led to soaring oil prices. This resulted in stagflation—high inflation and high unemployment—a combination that was challenging for many economies.

8.1.4 Early 1980s Recession:

A combination of tight monetary policies, high interest rates, and efforts to curb inflation led to a severe recession in the early 1980s in the United States and other parts of the world. Unemployment rates reached double digits in some countries.

8.1.5 Global Financial Crisis (2008-2009):

Triggered by the collapse of the housing market and the subsequent banking crisis, the 2008 financial crisis resulted in a severe worldwide economic downturn. Many businesses faced bankruptcy, and unemployment rates rose significantly in several countries.

8.1.6 COVID-19 Pandemic (2020):

The global COVID-19 pandemic led to widespread economic disruptions, business closures, and lockdowns. Many industries, particularly those in travel, hospitality, and entertainment, experienced significant job losses, leading to a global surge in unemployment.

8.1.7 Structural Unemployment (Various Periods):

Throughout history, there have been periods of structural unemployment caused by shifts in technology, changes in industries, and globalization. For example, the Industrial Revolution marked a transition from agrarian economies to industrialized ones, resulting in displacement and unemployment in certain sectors.

8.1.8 Austerity Measures (Various Periods):

Some periods of high unemployment can be linked to government policies, such as austerity measures aimed at reducing public spending. These measures, while intended to address economic challenges, can lead to job losses and economic contractions.

It's important to note that the causes of unemployment are often complex and multifaceted, involving a combination of economic, social, and political factors. Additionally, each historical period had unique circumstances that contributed to high unemployment rates. Policymakers, economists, and societies continually seek ways to mitigate these challenges and promote stable, inclusive economic growth.

8.2. How societies have overcome crises resulting from unemployment

Overcoming periods of enormous unemployment has been a challenge throughout history, and various strategies have been employed to address this issue. Here are some ways in which societies have sought to overcome high unemployment during different historical periods:

8.2. 1New Deal Programs (1930s - Great Depression):

In response to the Great Depression, U.S. President Franklin D. Roosevelt implemented the New Deal, a series of programs and policies aimed at providing relief, recovery, and reform. Programs like the Civilian Conservation Corps (CCC), Works Progress Administration (WPA), and the Tennessee Valley Authority (TVA) created jobs, built infrastructure, and supported economic recovery.

8.2.2 Post-World War II Reconstruction (1940s - Post-WWII):

After World War II, many countries, particularly in Europe and Japan, faced the task of rebuilding war-torn economies. Massive reconstruction efforts, including infrastructure projects and industrial revitalization, created jobs and contributed to post-war economic recovery.

8.2.3 Keynesian Economic Policies (Post-World War II):

The post-war period saw the adoption of Keynesian economic policies, which emphasized government intervention in the economy to manage demand. Governments used fiscal and monetary policies to stabilize economies and reduce unemployment.

8.2.4 Industrial Policy and Development (Various Periods):

In response to structural unemployment caused by shifts in technology and industry, governments have sometimes implemented industrial policies to promote new industries and technologies. This approach aims to create jobs in emerging sectors while helping workers transition from declining industries.

8.2.5 Counter-Cyclical Measures (Various Periods):

Governments often implement counter-cyclical measures during economic downturns to stimulate demand and employment. These measures may include fiscal stimulus packages, monetary easing, and targeted investments in key sectors.

8.2.6 Labor Market Reforms (Various Periods):

Some societies have undertaken labor market reforms to address structural unemployment. These reforms may include training and retraining programs, flexible labor market policies, and initiatives to match workers' skills with evolving industry needs.

8.2.7 Education and Skill Development (Ongoing):

Investing in education and skill development is a long-term strategy to address unemployment. By ensuring that the workforce is equipped with relevant skills, societies can adapt to changing economic conditions and foster innovation.

8.2.8 Global Cooperation (Post-World War II):

International collaboration and economic integration, as seen in institutions like the European Union, have played a role in promoting stability and reducing unemployment. Open trade and cooperation can lead to economic growth and increased job opportunities.

8.2.9 Technology and Innovation (Ongoing):

Advances in technology and innovation have created new industries and job opportunities. While automation can lead to job displacement in certain sectors, it has also contributed to the creation of new, often higher-skilled jobs.

8.2.10 Social Safety Nets (Ongoing):

Establishing robust social safety nets, including unemployment benefits, healthcare, and social assistance programs, can provide a financial cushion for individuals during periods of unemployment and contribute to economic stability.

It's important to note that overcoming unemployment requires a combination of short-term interventions and long-term structural changes. The specific strategies employed can vary based on the nature of the economic challenges and the social and political context of each period.

9

Unemployment and trends in healthcare

9.1 Health care in the jobless era

The future of healthcare in an age of unemployment is likely to undergo several changes and adaptations to address the evolving needs of individuals who may be facing unemployment. Here are some potential trends and considerations:

9.1.1 Telehealth and Remote Care:

Increased reliance on telehealth services to provide remote medical consultations, mental health support, and monitoring of chronic conditions. This can help bridge gaps in access to healthcare for those facing unemployment or financial constraints.

9.1.2 Mental Health and Well-being Focus:

Greater emphasis on mental health services and well-being programs, recognizing the psychological impact of unemployment. Integrating mental health support into primary care and community services can be a key aspect of future healthcare.

9.1.3 Community Health Initiatives:

Implementation of community-based healthcare initiatives to address the unique health needs of local populations. These initiatives may include mobile clinics, community health centers, and outreach programs to improve access to preventive and primary care services.

9.1.4 Health Education and Empowerment:

A focus on health education and empowerment to help individuals take control of their well-being. Healthcare providers may play a more active role in educating communities about preventive measures, healthy lifestyles, and self-care practices.

9.1.5 Workforce Training and Upskilling:

Initiatives to train and upskill healthcare workers to meet the changing demands of the healthcare landscape. This may include training programs for community health workers, telehealth professionals, and those involved in mental health support services.

9.1.6 Collaboration with Social Services:

Increased collaboration between healthcare providers and social services to address the social determinants of health, including unemployment, housing instability, and food insecurity. A holistic approach to healthcare may involve partnerships with organizations addressing these broader social issues.

9.1.7 Technology Integration for Accessibility:

Leveraging technology for enhanced healthcare accessibility. This could involve the use of mobile health apps, wearable devices, and other technologies to facilitate self-monitoring, health tracking, and timely interventions.

9.1.8 Financial Wellness Programs:

Integration of financial wellness programs within healthcare services. Recognizing the interconnectedness of financial and physical health, healthcare providers may offer resources and support to help individuals manage their financial well-being.

9.1.9 Preventive and Population Health Strategies:

Greater emphasis on preventive and population health strategies to reduce the burden on the healthcare system. This includes proactive measures such as vaccinations, health screenings, and lifestyle interventions to prevent the onset of chronic diseases.

9.1.10 Policy Changes and Advocacy:

Advocacy for policy changes to address healthcare disparities and promote equitable access to healthcare services. This may involve pushing for reforms that support universal healthcare, expanded insurance coverage, and improved access to affordable medications.

9.1.11 Innovation in Healthcare Delivery:

Continued innovation in healthcare delivery models, including value-based care, accountable care organizations, and other approaches that prioritize patient outcomes and cost-effectiveness.

9.1.12 Community Engagement and Empowerment:

Community engagement initiatives to involve individuals in their own healthcare decision-making. Empowering communities to actively participate in health promotion and prevention can lead to more sustainable and effective healthcare outcomes.

While the exact trajectory of healthcare in the age of unemployment will depend on various factors, these trends highlight potential directions that healthcare systems may take to address the evolving needs of populations facing unemployment. Collaboration between healthcare providers, policymakers, and communities will be essential to create a more resilient and inclusive healthcare ecosystem.

9.2 trends in psychological assistance

Psychologists can play a crucial role in addressing the psychological problems caused by automation at work. Here are some programs and interventions they can offer:

9.2.1 Resilience Training:

Develop resilience training programs to help individuals cope with the stress and uncertainties associated with automation. Focus on building psychological resilience, adaptability, and coping mechanisms to navigate workplace changes.

9.2.2 Career Transition Counseling:

Provide counseling services to individuals facing job displacement due to automation. Assist in exploring new career paths, identifying transferable skills, and developing strategies for successful career transitions.

9.2.3 Stress Management Workshops:

Conduct stress management workshops to address the anxiety and pressure that may arise from concerns about job security and changes in job roles. Teach stress reduction techniques, mindfulness, and relaxation methods.

9.2.4 Skill Development and Training Programs:

Collaborate with organizations to offer skill development and training programs. Equip employees with the skills necessary for the evolving job market, fostering a sense of competence and confidence in the face of change.

9.2.5 Change Management Support:

Assist organizations in implementing effective change management strategies. Help employees understand and embrace the changes brought about by automation, fostering a positive attitude toward innovation and adaptation.

9.2.6 Team Building and Communication Skills:

Offer team-building programs that focus on improving communication and collaboration within teams. Strengthening interpersonal skills can enhance workplace relationships and contribute to a positive work environment.

9.2.7 Career Coaching and Planning:

Provide individualized career coaching to help employees assess their strengths, values, and career goals. Assist in creating personalized career plans that align with the changing demands of the job market.

9.2.8 Wellness Programs:

Develop comprehensive wellness programs that address both physical and mental well-being. Incorporate elements such as fitness, nutrition, and mental health support to create a holistic approach to employee well-being.

9.2.9 Job Redesign and Job Crafting Workshops:

Explore job redesign and job crafting workshops to empower employees to proactively shape their roles within the organization. Encourage a sense of autonomy and personalization in job responsibilities.

9.2.10 Employee Assistance Programs (EAPs):

Implement or enhance Employee Assistance Programs to provide confidential counseling services, crisis intervention, and mental health support for employees facing challenges related to automation and job changes.

9.2.11 Digital Literacy Training:

Offer programs to enhance digital literacy skills. Help employees develop proficiency in using new technologies, tools, and platforms to ensure a smoother transition in the automated work environment.

9.2.12 Community Support and Networking:

Facilitate networking opportunities and support groups where employees can share experiences, provide mutual support, and build a sense of community. Establishing connections with others facing similar challenges can be reassuring.

9.2.13 Crisis Intervention and Mental Health First Aid:

Train managers and HR professionals in crisis intervention and mental health first aid. Equip them with the skills to identify signs of distress and provide initial support to those experiencing mental health challenges.

● ● ●

Psychologists can tailor these programs to the specific needs of individuals and organizations, fostering a proactive and supportive approach to addressing the psychological impact of automation at work.

10

Embracing Change

10.1 The Power of Adaptability

In the ever-changing landscape of the job market, adaptability has become a crucial skill for individuals to thrive in the jobless era. The ability to adapt to new technologies, industries, and work environments is essential for staying relevant and finding success in a world where traditional jobs are becoming obsolete. This section explores the power of adaptability and how it can be harnessed to navigate the challenges and opportunities of the jobless era.

The Need for Adaptability

As automation and artificial intelligence continue to advance, the job market is undergoing a significant transformation. Many traditional jobs are being replaced by machines, leading to a rise in unemployment rates. In this rapidly changing environment, individuals who are resistant to change and unwilling to adapt may find themselves left behind.

Adaptability is the key to survival in this new era. It allows individuals to embrace change, learn new skills, and explore emerging industries and opportunities. By being adaptable, individuals can position themselves to take advantage of the shifting job market and find new avenues for employment.

Embracing Continuous Learning

One of the fundamental aspects of adaptability is a commitment to lifelong learning. In a jobless era, where skills become outdated quickly, individuals must be willing to continuously acquire new knowledge and develop new skills. This can be achieved through formal education, online courses, workshops, or even self-directed learning.

By embracing continuous learning, individuals can stay ahead of the curve and remain competitive in the job market. They can acquire new skills that are in demand and adapt to the changing needs of industries. This not only increases their employability but also opens up new opportunities for career growth and advancement.

Flexibility and Versatility

Adaptability also involves being flexible and versatile in one's approach to work. In a jobless era, individuals may need to explore different industries, take on multiple roles, or even switch careers entirely. Being open to new experiences and willing to step outside of one's comfort zone can lead to exciting opportunities and personal growth.

● ● ●

Flexibility also extends to work arrangements. With the rise of remote work and the gig economy, individuals have the freedom to choose when, where, and how they work. Embracing this flexibility allows individuals to create a work-life balance that suits their needs and preferences.

Embracing Change and Taking Risks

Adaptability requires individuals to embrace change and be willing to take risks. It involves stepping into the unknown, trying new things, and being comfortable with uncertainty. This mindset allows individuals to seize opportunities that may arise in the jobless era and take calculated risks to pursue their goals.

By embracing change and taking risks, individuals can break free from the constraints of traditional employment and explore entrepreneurial ventures or self-employment. This can lead to greater autonomy, creativity, and fulfillment in their work.

Building Resilience

Adaptability is closely linked to resilience. In the face of adversity and setbacks, individuals who are adaptable can bounce back and find alternative paths to success. They are not deterred by failures but see them as opportunities for growth and learning.

Building resilience involves developing a positive mindset, cultivating strong problem-solving skills, and maintaining a sense of optimism. It allows individuals to navigate the challenges of the jobless era with confidence and perseverance.

Embracing Collaboration and Networking

In a jobless era, collaboration and networking become even more critical. By connecting with others in their field or industry, individuals can stay informed about emerging trends, share knowledge, and collaborate on projects. Networking also opens doors to new opportunities and potential partnerships.

Adaptable individuals understand the value of building relationships and actively seek out opportunities to connect with others. They engage in professional communities, attend conferences and events, and leverage social media platforms to expand their network.

Conclusion

Adaptability is the key to thriving in the jobless era. By embracing change, continuously learning, being flexible, and taking risks, individuals can position themselves for success in a rapidly evolving job market. Building resilience and fostering collaboration further enhance their ability to navigate the challenges and seize the opportunities that arise. In this era of uncertainty, adaptability is not just a skill; it is a mindset that empowers individuals to create a positive future for themselves.

10.2 Overcoming Fear and Resistance

In a world where automation and technology are rapidly transforming the job market, it is natural for individuals to experience fear and resistance. The idea of losing one's job to a machine or being unable to keep up with the changing demands of the workforce can be daunting. However, it is essential to understand that embracing change is crucial for personal growth and success in the jobless era.

Understanding the Fear

Fear is a natural response to the unknown, and the prospect of a jobless future can be overwhelming. People may fear losing their livelihoods, financial stability, and even their sense of identity tied to their professions. It is important to acknowledge these fears and understand that they are valid. However, dwelling on fear alone can hinder personal growth and prevent individuals from adapting to the changing landscape.

Embracing Change

Overcoming fear and resistance begins with embracing change. Instead of viewing automation and technology as threats, it is important to see them as opportunities for growth and innovation. By accepting that the job market is evolving, individuals can open themselves up to new possibilities and explore different avenues for success.

Developing a Growth Mindset

A growth mindset is a powerful tool in overcoming fear and resistance. It is the belief that one's abilities and intelligence can be developed through dedication and hard work. By adopting a growth mindset, individuals can view challenges as opportunities for learning and improvement. This mindset allows for the development of new skills and the ability to adapt to changing circumstances.

Embracing Lifelong Learning

In a jobless era, the importance of lifelong learning cannot be overstated. As technology continues to advance, new skills and knowledge become essential for staying relevant in the job market. By embracing lifelong learning, individuals can continuously acquire new skills, adapt to new technologies, and remain competitive in the workforce.

Seeking Support and Collaboration

Overcoming fear and resistance is not a journey that needs to be taken alone. Seeking support from peers, mentors, and professionals can provide valuable guidance and encouragement. Collaborating with others who are also navigating the jobless era can foster a sense of community and create opportunities for networking and skill-sharing.

Building Resilience

Resilience is the ability to bounce back from setbacks and adapt to change. In a jobless era, building resilience

● ● ●

is crucial for navigating the uncertainties of the future. Developing resilience involves cultivating a positive mindset, practicing self-care, and maintaining a strong support system. By building resilience, individuals can face challenges head-on and bounce back stronger than ever.

Embracing Entrepreneurship

One way to overcome fear and resistance is by embracing entrepreneurship. The jobless era presents a unique opportunity for individuals to create their own paths and pursue their passions. By starting a business or becoming self-employed, individuals can take control of their own destiny and create their own opportunities.

Embracing a Growth Mindset

In a jobless era, it is important to adopt a growth mindset. This mindset allows individuals to see setbacks as opportunities for growth and learning. By embracing a growth mindset, individuals can overcome fear and resistance and approach the future with optimism and a willingness to adapt.

Conclusion

Overcoming fear and resistance is essential for thriving in a jobless era. By embracing change, developing a growth mindset, and seeking support, individuals can navigate the uncertainties of the future with confidence. Embracing lifelong learning, building resilience, and considering entrepreneurship are all strategies that can help individuals overcome fear and resistance and create a positive future for themselves. The jobless era may be challenging, but with the right mindset and a willingness to adapt, individuals can find success and fulfillment in the changing world of work.

10.3 Embracing Lifelong Learning

In a rapidly changing job market, where automation and technology are replacing traditional jobs at an unprecedented rate, the need for lifelong learning has become more crucial than ever before. Lifelong learning refers to the continuous process of acquiring new knowledge, skills, and competencies throughout one's life. It is a mindset that embraces change and seeks personal and professional growth in order to adapt to the evolving demands of the job market.

10.3.1 The Importance of Lifelong Learning

Embracing lifelong learning is essential in a jobless era because it allows individuals to stay relevant and competitive in the face of technological advancements. As automation takes over routine and repetitive tasks, the demand for skills that are uniquely human, such as critical thinking, problem-solving, creativity, and emotional intelligence, is increasing. Lifelong learning enables individuals to develop and enhance these skills, making them more valuable in the job market.

Moreover, lifelong learning fosters adaptability and resilience. By continuously acquiring new knowledge and skills, individuals become more flexible and better equipped to navigate the changing job landscape. They can easily transition into new roles or industries,

●●●
151

mitigating the risk of unemployment. Lifelong learners are more likely to embrace change and see it as an opportunity for growth rather than a threat.

10.3.2 Strategies for Lifelong Learning

To effectively embrace lifelong learning, individuals need to adopt certain strategies that facilitate continuous growth and development. Here are some key strategies to consider:

10.3.2.1 Set Learning Goals

Start by setting clear learning goals. Identify the skills and knowledge you need to acquire or improve upon to remain relevant in your field or to explore new career opportunities. By having specific goals, you can structure your learning journey and measure your progress along the way.

10.3.2.2 Seek Diverse Learning Opportunities

Lifelong learning is not limited to formal education. Explore a variety of learning opportunities, including online courses, workshops, seminars, conferences, and networking events. Engage with experts in your field, join professional associations, and participate in communities of practice to expand your knowledge and gain insights from others.

10.3.2.3 Embrace Technology

Technology has revolutionized the way we learn. Take advantage of online platforms, educational apps, and digital resources to access a wealth of information and learning materials. Online courses, webinars, and virtual classrooms provide flexible and convenient options for acquiring new skills and knowledge.

10.3.2.4 Cultivate a Growth Mindset

Developing a growth mindset is crucial for lifelong learning. Embrace challenges, view failures as learning opportunities, and believe in your ability to learn and grow. Adopting a positive attitude towards learning will fuel your motivation and resilience, enabling you to overcome obstacles and achieve your learning goals.

10.3.2.5 Practice Reflective Learning

Reflective learning involves actively thinking about and analyzing your learning experiences. Regularly assess your progress, identify areas for improvement, and adjust your learning strategies accordingly. Reflecting on your learning journey helps consolidate knowledge, enhances self-awareness, and promotes continuous improvement.

10.3.3 Benefits of Lifelong Learning

Embracing lifelong learning offers numerous benefits that extend beyond professional growth. Here are some key advantages:

10.3.3.1 Personal Growth and Fulfillment

Lifelong learning allows individuals to pursue their passions and interests, leading to personal growth and fulfillment. By continuously expanding their knowledge and skills, individuals can explore new hobbies, develop new talents, and engage in lifelong intellectual stimulation.

10.3.3.2 Enhanced Employability

Continuous learning enhances employability by keeping individuals up-to-date with the latest industry trends and technological advancements. Employers value individuals who demonstrate a commitment to learning and self-improvement, making lifelong learners more attractive candidates for job opportunities.

10.3.3.3 Increased Adaptability

Lifelong learning equips individuals with the ability to adapt to changing circumstances and embrace new challenges. It enhances problem-solving skills, critical thinking abilities, and creativity, enabling individuals to navigate complex situations with confidence and agility.

10.3.3.4 Improved Cognitive Function

Engaging in lifelong learning has been linked to improved cognitive function and mental well-being. Learning new skills and acquiring knowledge stimulates the brain, enhances memory retention, and promotes overall cognitive health.

10.3.3.5 Social Connection and Networking

Lifelong learning provides opportunities for social connection and networking. Engaging in learning activities allows individuals to meet like-minded individuals, expand their professional networks, and collaborate on projects, fostering a sense of community and support.

10.3.4 Overcoming Barriers to Lifelong Learning

While lifelong learning offers numerous benefits, there can be barriers that hinder individuals from fully embracing it. Here are some common barriers and strategies to overcome them:

10.3.4.1 Time Constraints

Busy schedules and work commitments can make it challenging to allocate time for learning. Prioritize learning by creating a schedule and dedicating specific time slots for learning activities. Break down your learning goals into manageable tasks and consistently work towards them.

10.3.4.2 Financial Constraints

Some learning opportunities may come with a financial cost. However, there are often free or affordable alternatives available. Explore online resources, open educational platforms, and scholarships to access quality learning materials without breaking the bank.

10.3.4.3 Lack of Motivation

Maintaining motivation can be difficult, especially when faced with setbacks or slow progress. Find ways to stay motivated, such as setting rewards for achieving learning milestones, finding an accountability partner, or joining a study group. Celebrate your achievements along the way to keep your motivation high.

10.3.4.4 Fear of Failure

Fear of failure can prevent individuals from taking risks and pursuing new learning opportunities. Embrace a growth mindset and reframe failure as a stepping stone towards success. Remember that learning is a journey, and setbacks are natural and valuable learning experiences.

10.3.5 Conclusion

In a jobless era, lifelong learning is not just a choice but a necessity. By embracing lifelong learning, individuals can adapt to the changing job market, enhance their employability, and experience personal growth and fulfillment. It is a mindset that empowers individuals to navigate the uncertainties of the future with confidence and resilience. So, start your lifelong learning journey today and unlock a world of opportunities.

10.4 Creating a Positive Future

In a jobless era, where automation and technological advancements have rendered many traditional jobs obsolete, it is crucial to focus on creating a positive future. While the prospect of widespread unemployment may seem daunting, it also presents an opportunity for society to redefine work, explore new avenues of productivity, and foster a more fulfilling and meaningful existence. This chapter will delve into various strategies and approaches that can help us navigate this new landscape and shape a positive future for all.

● ● ●

10.4.1 Embracing Change and Innovation

Creating a positive future in a jobless era requires embracing change and fostering a culture of innovation. Instead of resisting technological advancements, individuals and societies should actively seek ways to adapt and leverage these advancements for the betterment of humanity. Embracing change involves being open to new ideas, exploring emerging technologies, and continuously learning and evolving. By embracing change, we can harness the power of innovation to create new opportunities and industries that align with the needs and aspirations of a jobless society.

10.4.2 Fostering Entrepreneurship and Collaboration

Entrepreneurship plays a vital role in creating a positive future in a jobless era. With traditional employment becoming scarce, individuals can explore entrepreneurship as a means of creating their own opportunities. Governments and organizations can support aspiring entrepreneurs by providing access to resources, mentorship programs, and funding opportunities. By fostering entrepreneurship, we can encourage creativity, innovation, and economic growth, while also empowering individuals to take control of their own destinies.

Collaboration is another key aspect of creating a positive future. In a jobless era, collaboration becomes even more critical as individuals and organizations need to work together to address societal challenges and create sustainable solutions. By fostering a

●●●

collaborative mindset, we can pool our collective knowledge, skills, and resources to tackle complex problems and create a more inclusive and equitable society.

10.4.3 Investing in Education and Skills Development

Education and skills development are essential for creating a positive future in a jobless era. As automation replaces many routine tasks, there is a growing need to equip individuals with the skills required for the jobs of the future. Education systems must adapt to emphasize critical thinking, problem-solving, creativity, and emotional intelligence. By investing in education and skills development, we can ensure that individuals are prepared to thrive in a rapidly changing job market.

Furthermore, lifelong learning becomes crucial in a jobless era. As technology continues to evolve, individuals must be willing to continuously update their skills and knowledge. Governments, organizations, and individuals should promote a culture of lifelong learning by providing accessible and affordable learning opportunities. This can include online courses, vocational training programs, and mentorship initiatives. By embracing lifelong learning, individuals can remain adaptable and resilient in the face of technological advancements.

10.4.4 Nurturing Well-being and Mental Health

Creating a positive future in a jobless era goes beyond economic considerations. It also involves nurturing well-being and prioritizing mental health. With traditional work structures changing, individuals may experience feelings of uncertainty, anxiety, and loss of purpose. It is crucial to provide support systems that address these challenges and promote overall well-being.

Society should prioritize mental health services, counseling, and community support networks. Additionally, individuals can cultivate practices such as mindfulness, self-care, and maintaining a healthy work-life balance. By nurturing well-being and mental health, we can create a society that values holistic success and happiness, rather than solely focusing on traditional employment metrics.

10.4.5 Redefining Success and Meaning

In a jobless era, it becomes imperative to redefine success and meaning. Instead of measuring success solely based on traditional employment and financial wealth, society should broaden its definition to encompass personal growth, contribution to the community, and overall well-being. By shifting the focus from materialistic pursuits to personal fulfillment and societal impact, we can create a more balanced and meaningful future.

Individuals can explore alternative paths to find purpose and meaning, such as volunteering, pursuing creative endeavors, or engaging in social activism. By aligning personal passions with societal needs, individuals can contribute to the betterment of society while finding personal fulfillment.

● ● ●

10.4.6 Building a Sustainable and Equitable Society

Creating a positive future in a jobless era requires building a sustainable and equitable society. As automation and technological advancements reshape the job market, it is crucial to ensure that the benefits are distributed fairly and that no one is left behind. Governments and organizations should prioritize policies that promote income equality, social safety nets, and access to basic necessities for all.

Additionally, sustainability should be at the forefront of our efforts. As we embrace new technologies and industries, we must prioritize environmental stewardship and work towards a greener and more sustainable future. By integrating sustainability into our economic and social systems, we can create a positive future that not only benefits individuals but also the planet as a whole.

In conclusion, creating a positive future in a jobless era requires embracing change, fostering entrepreneurship and collaboration, investing in education and skills development, nurturing well-being and mental health, redefining success and meaning, and building a sustainable and equitable society. By adopting these strategies, we can navigate the challenges of automation and technological advancements while creating a future that is inclusive, fulfilling, and prosperous for all.

Summary

● ● ●

● ● ●
163

●●●

● ● ●

165

● ● ●

♦ ♦ ♦

●●●

● ● ●

169

● ● ●